CW01559110

KEEPING IT REAL

KEEPING IT REAL

THE DARREN 'CHUCK' BERRY STORY

DARREN BERRY

WITH MARTIN BLAKE

Publishing

Published by:

Bas Publishing
ABN 30 106 181 542
F16/171 Collins Street
Melbourne Vic. 3000
Tel: (03) 9650 3200
Fax: (03) 9650 5077
Web: www.baspublishing.com.au
Email: mail@baspublishing.com.au

Copyright © 2004 Darren Berry & Martin Blake

This publication is copyright and may not be resold or reproduced in any manner (except excerpts thereof for bona fide study purpose in accordance with the Copyright Act) without the prior consent of the Publisher.

Every effort has been made to ensure that this book is free from error and/or omissions. No responsibility can be accepted by the Publisher, Author or any person involved in the preparation of this book for loss occasioned to any person acting or refraining from action as a result of material in this book.

The National Library of Australia Cataloguing-in-Publication entry:

Berry, Darren, 1969- .
    Keeping it real : the Darren 'Chuck' Berry story.

    ISBN 1 920910 33 6.

    1. Berry, Darren, 1969- . 2. Cricket players - Australia -
    Biography. 3. Cricket - Anecdotes. I. Blake, Martin. II.
    Title.

796.358092

Page Layout: exigene.com.au
Cover Design: Selina Low
Printed in Australia by Shannon Books

Cover photo: © The Herald & Weekly Times Photographic Collection

DEDICATION

*This book is dedicated to my parents, Roy and Norma Berry,
who sadly were both taken from me far too early in my life.
Their commitment towards me in my youth was incredible.
Time and time again they drove me from Wonthaggi in country
Victoria to Melbourne so I could chase my sporting dreams.
Without their efforts, my dreams may have never been fulfilled.*

ACKNOWLEDGEMENTS

I would like to thank Martin Blake from *The Age* newspaper in Melbourne for his time and patience in helping me to put this book together in a relatively short period of time.

Thanks to Bas Publishing and specifically David Tenenbaum for supporting our idea in writing this book. Also to Ross Dundas for supplying the statistical pages and to Garry Sparke, the official Cricket Victoria photographer, for allowing me to use some photos from his collection, and to the *Herald Sun* for access to their photo library.

Throughout my career I have been supported by two companies and two very special people in John Forbes (Puma Australia) and Greg Smyth (Gray Nicolls). Their generosity was most appreciated through good times and bad. Also to Jefferson Ford and Bolle sunglasses, for support at various stages of my career, I say thank you.

To all my teammates over the years, you were the reason I played the game, it was a pleasure to take the field with all of you. The support staff throughout the years with the Victorian team quite often lifted me and inspired me with their unrewarded commitment to the team's cause.

Finally to my wife Katherine, who has ridden every bump with me along the journey, and encouraged me to chase my dreams, your love and support means more to me than words can express.

Darren Berry

PREFACE

BY STEVE WAUGH

In any era of cricket there is always a stand out performer who for one reason or another doesn't get the ultimate reward that he deserves, the chance to wear the baggy green.

Darren 'Chuck' Berry is one such example because there is no doubt in my mind he would have been a star at the highest level. Not that you'd tell Chuck that! For one, he's a Victorian, and secondly you'd create a monster that was always lurking just beneath the surface.

Seriously though, if I had to pick the three best gloveman I've played with and against, I'd nominate without hesitation Ian Healy, Jack Russell and Darren Berry and be unable to split the trio.

Each had the innate ability and sixth sense of being in the right position to execute a dismissal, where others hesitate and don't anticipate. Darren was a freak up to the stumps off the quick men, performing miracle stumpings, memorable sledges and knockabout Aussie humour whilst also managing to fidget and readjust his clothing and cap like an obsessive compulsive addict.

He was always a team man through and through, and as an opposition player you always respected that trait. Regularly he would stand up for his team and fellow players in the hope of inspiring them, often leaving himself open to the aggression and frustration of the opposition as a consequence. The 'Blues' certainly loved the sometimes prickly in-your-face attitude he exhibited, and often we'd buy into the banter and gamesmanship Chuck thrived on. The mention from a Blues fielder that the custodian's pants size looked like it had gone from a 34 to a 36 from the previous season would certainly get a swift turn of the head to see who was dangling the bait out. It was then 'game-on' and the ensuing battle was always a titanic struggle, based around personal pride.

I always enjoyed lining up against Chucky boy and the Vics because it was always played hard and fair. Chuck, I can say I would have also loved to have had the honour of sharing a Baggy Green with you.

Well played Chuck – a great career and one that you can be very proud of.

Steve Waugh

Contents

FOREWORD

BY SHANE WARNE

When Chuck asked me to write the foreword to his book, I agreed straight away. Chuck and I have been friends for 15 years, and I'm honoured to do this. We have shared so many good times together. Off the field, our wives are good friends; we have shared many pies, beers, hangovers and sore throats supporting our beloved Saints in the AFL over the years, and hey, that's not over yet. On the field, we have played together for the Vics for 15 years, I stood along side him at slip, we toured together for Australia on a couple of occasions, and there should have been more. He's spent years standing behind the stumps to my bowling, so it would be fair to say we have plenty in common.

Chuck is a very loyal friend, no matter what the situation or where in the world we might be. He is always in contact to let me know what is going on in Australia and just to say "hi", although lately I feel I should send him a couple of bucks in the post for the cost of a call, now that he is hobnobbing it with the MMM team in his radio commentary, and doing a very good job may I say.

Chuck has been an inspiration to all of us who wanted to become the best cricketer we could be. In fact he would probably be the most passionate cricketer I have ever played with. Some people misunderstood his passion, but his heart was always in the right spot. As far as his wicketkeeping ability goes, to me he is the best gloveman I have seen standing up to the stumps bar none, and I don't say that because this is his book, or because he is my friend. I know there are a lot of other players in Australian cricket who feel the same way.

Chuck was unlucky that in his era he had Ian Healy who did unbelievably well for Australia and then Adam Gilchrist who, along with the Zimbabwean Andy Flower, was the best batsman-wicketkeeper in our time. Some of Chuck's stumpings off the slow bowlers were brilliant, and those who played with him will never forget the one he created off Paul Reiffel's bowling down the leg-side to remove David Boon at the MCG. Chuck really was unbelievably good at what he did, and it would have been nice for him to have a chance to play a Test match. But you never heard him complaining about it, which was a sign of the type of guy he is. Chuck is a caring person and the most important things to him are his family and close friends and at the end of the day, we're all the same in that.

The boy from Wonthaggi has had a wonderful career in cricket, and has been a great friend for a long time. I wish he, Kath and his young daughter Jordan a great future. Knowing Chuck the way I do, this will be a book well worth the read. I hope that it's a hit, mate, and I'll see you soon. Your friend, Warnie.

Shane Warne

INTRODUCTION

BY MARTIN BLAKE

Let me tell you a couple of things about Darren 'Chuck' Berry.

You don't really need to hear me talk ad nauseum about his wicketkeeping. Like a lot of people in and around the edges of cricket, I know little about this mysterious art, practised by a fraction of the people who play the game. I would compare it with my knowledge of wine. Which is to say, simply, that you just know when you've got a good one.

Chuck was a good one all right. The ball melted into his gloves. When he came up to the stumps, always the telltale sign with keepers, he looked just as much at home as when he was standing back. In fact more so.

I have no doubt Chuck was a world class cricketer throughout his career, and he became one of the great characters of the domestic game in Australia, where cricket is tougher than anywhere on the planet. In another era Chuck might well have played 50 Tests for Australia; in his own time he could have walked into any one of various Test teams and donned the gloves. Don't doubt me on this. Just read Steve Waugh's words about Chuck on another page of this book.

But there is only one wicketkeeper in any team, and Chuck never extracted that elusive Test match he craved, a dream unfulfilled. Chuck believed in aiming high and right to the end, even when others – myself included – had given up hope, he was still believing, still anxiously awaiting those announcements of Australian touring teams on the radio and on television. He is still inclined to search for reasons for this, blaming his inconsistent batting or his occasional tiffs with administrators. But really, we don't need to look any farther than the names of the people who were ahead of him in the pecking order to find the explanation.

Ian Healy was first picked for Australia in 1988 and stayed until 1999, establishing himself as one of the game's all-time greats. Healy was not only a great keeper and a fine lower-order batsman, he was a warrior who refused to succumb to the minor inconvenience of injuries. Plainly he followed Dennis Lillee's cricket maxim of "never give a sucker an even break". He missed a single Test match in all that time, at Lahore in 1994 when the selectors brought the New South Welshman Phil Emery into the team, narrowly pipping Chuck for the spot.

By the time Healy departed with a helping hand from the national selectors, a chap named Adam Gilchrist was 27 and had been waiting several years for a baggy, green cap. Gilchrist had already made a name as an astonishingly powerful opening batsman in one-day cricket. His elevation to the Test team was overdue, and he will surely go down as one of the game's all-time champions, like Healy. Between that pair they have covered nearly 20 years of wicketkeeping for Australia. Which shows that in life, timing is everything.

It's a moot point as to whether Chuck ought to have gone on a few tours as reserve keeper. He did play a few matches for Australia on the Ashes tour of 1997 when Gilchrist broke down. He played in Sheffield Shield and Pura Cup triumphs 14 seasons apart, skippering the second of those. He played in a couple of national one-day championships with his beloved Victoria, including one as captain.

He played more games for his state than anyone and affected more dismissals than anyone by a street. This is some sort of career by any measure.

I watched it all with admiration from the press box. Chuck didn't believe in the wall that separates the players and the press. I clearly remember him summoning me over to his table at breakfast in our hotel in Perth one day during a match years ago, and chiding me for thinking that I ought to sit alone. I never totally agreed with him on this, and the journo in me was screaming at me to keep my distance. But I admired him for the thought, because I can assure you that forming friendships with the press is not the ticket to popularity within the team.

We did become friends, but not until much later, until the catastrophic 1995-96 season when he was dumped from the team for half a season. In 20 years of covering cricket I've never seen such a politically-charged, ill-conceived and disastrous non-selection and I said so in my newspaper, *The Age*. I copped my share of flak, as did everyone in that awful episode, which is covered in detail in these pages. I did it because I thought it was wrong, because I knew that Chuck was the heart and soul of the team and that the decision would cause unrest. I didn't do it because I liked Chuck. But he appreciated it all the same.

Which is not to say that Chuck was incapable of the odd spray in my direction. I recall one early-morning phone call at home during a Sheffield Shield match after Victoria had endured a dreadful day and I'd launched into an untimely attempt at satire in my morning article, borrowing from the famous line from the English writer Martin Johnson: "There are only three things wrong with Victoria. They can't bat, bowl or field." Chuck didn't like it and upon reflection, I didn't either. I gave up on satire. He said what he had to say, and we moved on.

That's the Chuck Berry I came to know and like immensely. It would have been easy for him to pack it all in at various stages. Instead, he stayed and recorded some monumental achievements. It is these achievements, rather than what might not have happened, that we have endeavoured to celebrate most in this book.

Martin Blake

CHAPTER 1   TRIUMPH

*Hearts to hearts and hands to hands, beneath the blue and
white we stand,*
We'll shout: 'God Bless Our Native Land'. Victoria ... Victoria,
Out they come, out they come, out they come to play,
Not just for recreation's sake, nor pass the time away,
Lots of fun, heaps of fun, enjoy yourself today,
Victorian boys are hard to beat when they come out to play.
So join in the chorus, and sing it one and all,
Join in the chorus, Victoria's on the ball,
Good old Victoria, they're winners you'll agree,
Victoria will be champions, just you wait and see.
— Victorian team song

The sound of bat brushing ball. A catch offered low to the
right-hand side of the keeper, gloved cleanly in both hands, and
the ball clutched in to his body rather than hurled to the sky in
the usual, demonstrative way. Joe Dawes, Queensland's fast
bowler and tail-end batsman, is out, caught Darren Berry bowled
Mick Lewis, and Victoria has won the Pura Cup (nee Sheffield
Shield) for the first time in 14 seasons.

The next three minutes are bordering on the surreal. I can't
hear anything, yet there is a din around me. Victoria's players

form a pack and someone grabs me away from the bunch for a television interview. I can't speak properly. The interview is garbage. My wife, Kath, comes down on to the ground, which she never does as a general rule. She is one of two or three people who know that I have just completed my last game of first class cricket. I gather my thoughts for long enough to embrace her and our baby daughter, Jordan, and I place the ball in Kath's pocket, telling her to make sure she doesn't let anyone take it from her.

I embrace Greg Shipperd, our coach, who has stood in since the horrific incident that had caused David Hookes' death a few months earlier. Shipperd has done it tough, tougher than most, for he was very close to Hookes. We're very emotional. There's the trophy to be accepted and 8000 or so fans in the stands. I pay my tribute to Hookes and to John Scholes, our previous coach, who had also died prematurely and tragically the previous year.

Is this the moment to announce my retirement? I've kept it from the boys all week, not wanting to impact upon the game in any way. "Not many sportsmen get to end their career with a fairytale," I tell the crowd, and out in front of me, I can hear Barb, a well-known and long-time Victorian supporter, saying: "Nooo." I tell everyone that I've played my last game, snared my last catch. It's hard to say, and a couple of players are shocked. Jon Moss asks: "What have you done?" Some of them think that it has come on the spur of the moment, but the opposite is the case.

So into the dressing rooms beneath the cavernous Great Southern Stand. There is Victorian memorabilia all around the whitewashed walls of the room. Matthew Elliott, whom I anointed several years earlier to lead our anthem, calls everyone to order. We gather in a circle, but as per our arrangement, we leave a space in it, just near Hookesy's locker. The space is for him.

We belt out the song and there are contrasting emotions flying around. Relief, that at the end of a season we had dominated, we are able to finish it in style in the final. Elation at the victory and the fact we've been able to do it for Hookesy and for ourselves. Tears for a few. Mathew Inness missed out on the final in a split vote, a heartbreaking situation for a player who had been with the side almost all through the season. I had the job of telling him the selectors' decision before the game, a task that didn't come easily. I voted to retain him in the side, but I was the only one. As is the custom, the selectors' vote has to be seen to be solid and I had to tell him so.

There has been the impact of Hookes' death outside a St Kilda hotel in January. Personally I've had to deal with distraught, young players who couldn't sleep at night any more, not to mention my own grief at the loss of a friend. I've had to front a media conference as captain to tell the world how the team was feeling about the loss of our coach, a trial that took every bit of emotional energy that I possess. He has been a mentor to me in my efforts to move into the media in the latter part of my career, and a long-time friend. And we've all had to put it to one side and get on with our jobs.

For me, there is redemption. I've played 14 years for my state and been thrown out of the team for half a season a few years earlier on grounds that I considered to be spurious and largely political, left standing on top of a hill at Apollo Bay trying to extract scores from a game in Perth in which I'm not playing, struggling for mobile phone reception to get the news and wondering whether life is worth living. I've come back into the team and seen others depart. I've broken a finger during my first season as full-time captain and needed eight weeks of rehabilitation to get into a position where I can play, scarcely ideal for a team-leader. A few weeks before the final, I've been summoned to the offices of Cricket Victoria and told that I should resign the captaincy because I've sworn loudly in the dressing rooms at Adelaide Oval and been reported, just a few days after my coach's funeral service. When I've declined to resign, the administration has told me it has no option but to sack me, only to withdraw a couple of days later.

There has been the birth of my first child in October the previous year, an event that has changed my perspective on life. Previously, I have lived for cricket, my great passion. Now I have realised that cricket is not life and death.

All this has been tossed around in my mind, and the row with my employers has tipped me over the edge. I've decided to hang up the gloves. I've discussed it with my wife and one or two close friends. I've approached David Boon, a national selector, and asked him straight out if I am kidding myself that I might one day wear the baggy, green cap. For 25 years or more I've lived this dream of playing for Australia and, save for a few games filling in for an injured Adam Gilchrist on the England tour of 1997, it hasn't happened. Boon tells me that it's not going to happen; that my batting has cost me, plus the fact that I've missed so much cricket in recent times because of the finger injury. There's always an excuse ready. In all my time for Victoria, I've never even been picked for an Australia 'A' game, when many other state keepers have had the luxury. It rankles.

The national selectors have just picked a team for a tour of Sri Lanka and named Wade Seccombe, of Queensland, as back-up wicketkeeper. Seccombe is a keeper I admire for his catching especially, but not so much as an up-to-the-stumps gloveman. If he's ever kept to a leg-spinner, then I'm not aware of it. Yet Australia goes to Sri Lanka with two leg-spinners, Shane Warne and Stuart MacGill, and picks Seccombe as the second keeper. I've kept to Warne my whole career. It tells me that I'm not in the frame. I've chased that dream and not for one minute really believed that I wouldn't achieve it. Until now, and it hits me that I won't.

I've thought about whether I can play on for Victoria. But I look around and the old names have gone. Merv Hughes, Tony Dodemaide, Jamie Siddons, Simon O'Donnell, Dean Jones, Paul Reiffel, Damien Fleming, they've all gone now. There's a new breed of players who've moved through, guys who take ice baths and drink Powerade and go home early after a day's play, where I'd be more inclined to sit around having a beer and chatting, always the last to leave.

Physically and mentally I'm cooked at 34. Could I eke out another couple of years? Yes, I could. But can I stand another pre-season running around Melbourne's famous Tan track? No, I can't. Am I prepared to do what's required at this level, getting up at six in the morning for weight sessions and extra practice after 15 years. No, I'm not. They say that the decision comes to sportsmen like a light turning on, and it's true. I just know that it's time for someone else to chase the dream.

I remember back to a few years ago when Robert Walls, a former AFL footballer and coach, came and spoke to the group about where we were heading and what we wanted to achieve in our sporting careers. He posed an interesting question to the boys that stuck in my mind and also helped my decision making process to retire. He asked: "What's the difference between commitment and involvement?" The answer was that being involved is giving 100% when you feel like it, whereas being committed was to give 100%, 100% of the time. I always believed I was committed and did not want to finish my career just being involved.

The last day of the final arrives and the championship is already ours. Queensland needs to win to take the trophy away and we only need a draw, a formality once we batted for the first three days. Eight wickets today will give us the outright victory we crave. Driving up Richmond's Bridge Road toward the ground in the morning, the MCG's light towers come into view. I've got one of my favourite songs, Bruce Springsteen's 'Glory Days' on the stereo system in the car and Victoria's captain is a blubbering mess. *"Glory days, they will pass you by, glory days, in the wink of a young girl's eye!"* croons The Boss. I pull over and ring Kath and she shepherds me through. *"Don't be an idiot! Enjoy yourself!"* she says.

The opponent is significant to us. Queensland has caused us so much pain over the years, twice denying us in finals in Brisbane in controversial circumstances. Sections of the media are criticising the way we have played the final, batting on beyond 700 in the first innings. So we are desperate for vindication; we want the outright win.

But it's a wearing, fifth-day wicket and I draw the guys together and copy a ploy that John Scholes had utilised in a grade final a few years earlier. I put my hand in the middle of the circle and asked them in turn to put theirs in as well. "Are we in this together, and will we walk off the field without a win?" I'm emotional and I can see tears welling in a few players' eyes. "Everyone knows what we've been through, losing John Scholes and David Hookes. Let's go out there and win this game for John Scholes, for David Hookes, but above all else let's go out and win this for Victoria, and for this 12 players here, and for the whole squad who've been part of it!"

At this moment I know that we cannot lose. And the job is done by that afternoon.

So we sing the song that I proposed that we sing five years earlier, borrowing heavily from the anthem used by Victorian teams when Australian football still had the State-of-Origin concept, and Ted Whitten ruled. My head is almost exploding at this point since I know I won't sing it again.

As usual I'm last out of the rooms that night, around midnight, and I leave my bag there to collect. Three days later I go back to the MCG to pick it up, and the security man lets me in the rooms. And all the balloons and streamers and cricket memorabilia and photographs of state record-holders and legends have gone and the walls are stark, plain white again, just in time for the football season. I pick up the bag and walk down the tunnel into the car park and I know that nothing's permanent.

Time to move on.

CHAPTER 2 THE PADDOCK

Cricket started for me in what became affectionately known as The Paddock.

It was our MCG, make no mistake. But in reality, it was just a big, vacant house block at the end of Catalpa Street, Doveton, where I grew up, an unpretentious, working-class deep eastern suburb of Melbourne.

My mates and I played with a tennis ball, taped up on one side so that it would swing for the quicker bowlers. We mowed and rolled the pitch and marked out the boundaries for our 'Test' matches, which were epics lasting a week at a time.

It is a familiar Australian story. These matches were an everyday event after school at Doveton West Primary School, and they were only ever ended by the call of a mother when the sun had begun to set. I can still hear my Mum yelling: "Darren! Dinner's on the table." If the match had not been completed, we simply wrote the progress scores on the fence and picked it up again the next day.

I was around seven years old when I joined in these matches, a few years younger than most of the other boys, all of whom lived in my neighbourhood. My mates included Rodney and Warren

Peake, who lived opposite me, Henry Torres up on the corner, Rodney Bowman, Ray Spinks, Jim Davey from the bottom of the Magnolia St hill and my closest friend back then Robbie Boorer, who had a mop of hair that resembled Ronnie Wearmouth, a Collingwood football superstar of that era. In football season, it was "jumpers down" for the goalposts, and the matches again lasted until darkness sent us scurrying inside. Later, we dug holes and installed goalposts at each end.

Football in winter; cricket in summer. Now there's an Australian story. It was my life.

Usually in this type of cricket, kids will use the back fence to stop the ball that passes the bat. A million backyard matches in Australia have been played with a trampoline turned on its side and strategically placed behind the stumps to serve as wicketkeeper.

But not in our games. Right from the start, I wanted to get in behind the stumps. The other boys worshipped Australia's demonic fast bowler Dennis Lillee and Ian Chappell, the captain and No. 3 batsman. But Rod Marsh, our great wicketkeeper, was my hero. I would stand up to the stumps to take the ball in my bare hands, despite the unpredictable bounce and the fact some of the kids were four or five years older and stronger than me.

No one ever taught me how to wicketkeep. I learned from watching on television. When I was about 10, my mother bought me a pair of red, Rod Marsh Kookaburra gloves which became my most treasured possession. I still have those battered gloves. Quite clearly my path had been set.

My father Lindin Roy Berry (known as Roy) was a carpenter in nearby Dandenong. Dad had also served in the Australian Navy in World War II. He and my mother, Norma Fay Berry, moved to Melbourne from Tasmania in the early years of their marriage.

They had four children – eldest brother Ron, sisters Dianne and Vicki and brother Lindin – over a six-year period and then 17 years later, when Dad was 50 and Mum 42, I came along. Clearly I was one of those little accidents, but I was very close to my parents growing up, as I did, as the only child still at home. I used to cop stick at school about their age – "Here comes your Nan and Pop to pick you up" — and I was very defensive of them.

Dad had not been a cricketer but he did play football and was a Tasmanian boxing champion. Mum had been a dressmaker and was also a more-than-handy pastry cook who at one stage ran her own cake shop, but had stopped working by the time I came along. My elder sister Dianne was an outstanding swimmer who was asked to trial for the 1968 Olympic Games in Mexico City. She declined the chance as she felt her shoulders were getting too big and she was concerned how that would disrupt her social meetings with the opposite sex.

Dad was deaf in one ear from the guns on HMAS Vampire, a fact I used to exploit with a few well-chosen words from the appropriate side as a cocky youngster. But I was lucky to have their total attention, and my brothers and sisters used to call the backyard 'Toy World' when I was a boy. They were jealous of the attention I received, and felt I was spoiled. Of course they were right.

One of the much older kids who played at The Paddock, Ray Spinks, played cricket for Buckley Ridges, a club in Dandenong. When I was about eight, he took me down to the cricket ground for a more formal game with my first club. "I'm a wicketkeeper," I told them. "We've already got a wicketkeeper," I was promptly told. "You're too small."

So I started bowling leg-spinners. I can guarantee that I was no threat to Shane Warne, let me tell you, and I wasn't happy that I could not don the gloves. But I played a couple of seasons for Buckley Ridges under 12s, learning what all wicketkeepers come to know: that sometimes, you have to wait. We played on malthoid wickets and I remember once we were bowled out for 9! Batting at number 11, my six not out was the stand out innings and top score!

I did learn the importance of cricket's traditions and Buckley Ridges gave me my first cricket cap, a dark blue and light blue number which I loved. When my brother Lindin took me to see my first live match, a World Series Cricket encounter between Australia and the West Indies at Waverley Park in 1979, I ran on to the ground at the end of the game and some idiot swiped it from me. I bawled my eyes out that night.

I was 10 years old and my brother couldn't understand why I was so upset about a cap. But it was so much more than that to me.

Oh yes, and The Paddock? I used to go back there every year and soak up the memories until about 10 years ago when I was shattered to find it had been paved over and made into a car park for the local scout hall. Which goes to show that the times move. Things were about to move for me, as well.

CHAPTER 3 WONTHAGGI

When I was 10 and in fifth grade at school, my father retired and the family moved to the small, South Gippsland town of Wonthaggi, 150 kilometres east of Melbourne. This was a flashpoint for me in several ways.

I thought Doveton was the centre of the whole world. All my mates were there. Everything I needed was there. But Mum and Dad wanted to go to the country and be close to the beach, and the little house at 41 Parkes Street, Wonthaggi, would become our home.

These were difficult times for a 10-year-old. I was on the receiving end of a barrage of teasing at my new school. I was regarded as a 'city-slicker', and I was goaded about the age of my parents. I got into a lot of fights over that.

I reckon it took until halfway through grade six for me to win any sort of acceptance and it was sport that did the trick for me. It broke down the barriers.

I started playing under 16 cricket on a Saturday morning for North Wonthaggi. Brett Lovett, who would later become an AFL footballer for Melbourne, was one of my teammates. Soon afterward I switched to East Wonthaggi, where I came across my first real cricket coach, Colin Bolding, who ran the club. I told him I was a keeper. "Good," he said. "We're looking for a 'keeper."

Colin was a great influence and things began to happen for me. I was playing in an after-school competition on Friday nights, juniors on Saturday mornings, and when I was 12, started playing 'B Grade' with the men on Saturday afternoons as well, at the suggestion of Bolding, who played on Saturday afternoons for my senior club, Wonthaggi Rovers.

My first captain in the Rovers' 'B Grade' team was Malcolm Conn, who became an award-winning cricket writer for *The Australian* newspaper a few years later. What I remember from those times is that when I stood up to the stumps, even to the supposedly quicker bowlers, the men couldn't believe it. "What are you doing?" they'd ask.

What I was doing was what I had learned in The Paddock, where the proximity of the fence didn't allow me the luxury of standing back. I was starting to take some strides as a keeper. Bert Matcott was the father of one of my teammates, and he had played as a wicketkeeper for Carlton in Melbourne District (nowadays called Premier) cricket. I distinctly remember him saying: "Son. You're going a long way with your keeping. You're the best young keeper I've ever seen."

I began to love Wonthaggi, which was a typically sports-driven country town. I played football with Rovers as an on-baller, captaining the under-14 team to a premiership; graduating to the senior team at 15. The town revolved around the football club. In summer, the local newspaper was full of cricket. I played golf (poorly), badminton, basketball, underwater hockey, in fact anything that was going. My plans were clear: I wanted to play cricket for Australia and league football for St Kilda.

Ian Harvey, who would become an all-rounder for Australia at international level, lived across the fence and his elder brother, Darren, became a friend of mine. In our long-winded cricket matches in the Harvey family driveway, Ian and his two younger brothers Craig and Chad were scouts for myself and Darren, chasing the ball all over the place.

As a kid, I never minded taking on older and bigger boys in sport. It is something that stayed with me: that confidence, that inner drive, call it what you will. I had some ambition and it was about being the best I could be, driving myself and testing myself to get there. Which is why, after my first cricket season with Rovers, I changed clubs because they did not have an 'A grade' team, moving to Dalyston a tiny town on the outskirts of Wonthaggi. Bert encouraged me to take the step, and Rovers did not stand in my way.

Then after one season at Dalyston, I moved again, this time to the exotically-named Outtrim-Moyarra-Kongwak Cricket Club in the Leongatha association. This was a somewhat controversial move, since Leongatha was half an hour away and in some ways, the arch-enemy of Wonthaggi.

I was head-hunted for the job by Steve McNamara, captain-coach of Outtrim, opening batsman and a legend of the area in his own right. I was 14 when he came knocking at the door, asking me to open the batting with him. Had Don Bradman turned up at home I'd hardly have been more excited.

So that year I played juniors in the morning and opened the batting with McNamara at Leongatha in the afternoons, getting a few 60s and 70s. One of my friends, Rob Coldabella, who was playing at Outtrim went down to Melbourne to play third-eleven cricket with Ringwood, one of the District teams, and as it happened, I went down to training with him.

I ended up wicketkeeping for Ringwood's Dowling Shield (under 16) team two years in a row, winning the competition in the first year. The Dowling Shield was the top under 16 competition in the state and was regarded as a nursery for state players. My appearance sparked the usual comments around the club: "Who's this kid from the bush who stands up to the opening bowlers?"

It was becoming obvious that I had a chance to play District cricket, the competition just one step underneath the Sheffield Shield—the vaunted national championship and the best domestic cricket competition in the world by popular consensus. But Michael Dimattina, Victoria's wicketkeeper in the Shield competition, was the senior keeper at Ringwood. Which meant that I would have been banging my head against a brick wall had I chosen Ringwood as my club.

Fate stepped in here. I was picked as the keeper for the Victorian under 16 team, which went to Perth for a national championship. Our coach was Doug Rumble, who was Fitzroy's first-eleven wicketkeeper, and we two glovemen naturally bonded. Towards the end of the carnival he said to me: "You're the best young keeper I've seen. Come to Fitzroy, and we'll start you in the seconds. I've only got a year or two left in me, and you can take over."

I had every intention of taking him up on the offer but a while later, things changed again. Back in Wonthaggi, I read in the paper one day that Rumble had been killed in a snow skiing accident. George Murray, a decorated coach and state under-age selector from Fitzroy/Doncaster rang me, and said: "Darren, Doug Rumble's been killed. He told me you're the best young keeper he's seen. We want you to play in the firsts for us."

Doug Rumble was killed trying to save his wife from going over a ledge, an indescribable tragedy. But he left a legacy for me

CHAPTER 4 ADELAIDE

The Australian Institute of Sport's cricket academy, for a long time based in Adelaide but recently moved to Brisbane, has been hailed as one of the primary reasons for our country's rise to the top of the tree in cricket. It's a notion that I happen to agree with.

I was part of the first intake of 16 young cricketers in 1988, and that year changed my outlook forever.

By this time, I was earning some plaudits for my keeping and I had represented Victoria three times at the national under 19 titles, the last of those as captain. I had also been picked for the Australian team to contest the first Youth World Cup in February-March 1988 in the Riverina district, with the final to be played in Adelaide.

Australia won the cup under the captaincy of another Victorian, Geoff Parker, who was a schoolboy superstar. In the final at the famous Adelaide Oval, we defeated a Pakistan team which boasted Inzamam ul-Haq, a burly batsman who would become one of the best in the world soon enough.

The cricket was high quality. Three of the captains – Mike Atherton (England), Brian Lara (West Indies) and Lee Germon (New Zealand) – went on to skipper their teams at senior level.

These were heady times for a kid from Wonthaggi, by far my biggest thrill to that point, and I had 27 dismissals in eight matches for the tournament without conceding a bye.

It was an opportunity to showcase what I had, and it helped that Jack Potter, a former Victorian player who coached that Australian Youth team, would be appointed as the first coach of the AIS academy in Adelaide. Potter was effectively on a spying mission for the ambitious project he was about to head up.

Soon after the World Cup I received an invitation to join the academy, set up by the Australian Cricket Board as a finishing school for talented young players. It was the opportunity of a lifetime, but what the invitation did was force me to make a decision.

To this point of my life, I'd fancied myself as a footballer on equal terms to my cricket. In the previous year I'd played two games for my beloved St Kilda in the club's under 19 team, on a VFL country permit. I was a ruck-rover, changing at half-forward with Nathan Burke, which I've often said is my claim to fame as a footballer. Burke, of course, went on to be a club legend but for those few games he had to wait for me to come off the ball for a break!

St Kilda, coached by Graeme Gellie, was enduring some of its toughest times in the seniors and 'Blind Freddie' could see that there were opportunities to be had for an ambitious young footballer. I was only 17, but I had been invited to train with the senior group and I'd been on a camp at Lake Eildon with the Saints along with the likes of Stewart Loewe, who like Burke, became a club legend and captain.

But cricket made the decision for me by offering me a chance to go to the academy. I was already making national youth teams and I can remember having an important conversation with

Brian Taber, the former Australian Test wicketkeeper who happened to manage the Youth team. I told Taber about the football situation and he said: "I reckon you're good enough with the gloves to go all the way."

Even in those days, it had become impossible to pursue both sports at the highest level like some people had done before. To make it in cricket, I would need to commit to 12 months full-time in Adelaide at the academy to begin with, not to mention what was to come after that. I had no guarantees at St Kilda, so I told them I'd be sticking with my cricket.

Hindsight tells me it was the correct decision, although I've pondered it sometimes. My wicketkeeping was going well, and I'd made a century in a Youth Test for Australia against a New Zealand team that included the outstanding all-rounder Chris Cairns. But my gut feel was that for my height (180 centimetres), I lacked some pace to make it at AFL level. Had I stayed at St Kilda and worked on it, who knows? I chose cricket and I have no regrets.

I can remember Mum's tears as I left home in my Ford Escort panel van and drove to Adelaide early in 1988, leaving my parents in an empty nest, the last child to depart the family home. It was a big move for me, even though there were three other Victorians in the squad – Geoff Parker, Ian Frazer and Brian McFadyen. I was the youngest in the squad at 18 and I was homesick two months into the trip. I missed my parents, and I'm sure I wasn't the only one in that group who was feeling the pinch.

But soon enough I began to warm to Adelaide, which I thought of as a big country town. The first intake had the likes of Stuart Law, the outstanding Queensland batsman, Jamie Cox from Tasmania, Joe Scuderi, an all-rounder from upcountry Queensland and Adrian Tucker, from New South Wales, who to that point was the best leg-spinner I had seen.

We lived in student accommodation at St Mark's College, part of Adelaide University and right next to our training base at Adelaide Oval. It was a sensational environment for a young bloke. We looked upon ourselves as university students without the unnecessary distraction of studies, although when we rose at 6am for our weight sessions we were known to cross paths with students still partying, a disparity in lifestyles that caused a certain amount of tension. Then again, we'd sometimes been known to slide into those parties as interlopers.

We practised in the nets at Adelaide Oval and our gymnasium was at the university, where a fitness trainer named Bob Crouch introduced us to the Versa-climber—a piece of equipment that was considered revolutionary back then. Crouch had trained Chris Dittmar, the champion squash player, and he did not spare us. It was some of the hardest training I can remember.

The scholarship-holders all were allocated an Adelaide club for our weekend cricket, and both Law and I went to Tea Tree Gully, a new club that had been struggling. Law and I played together and developed a friendship which manifested itself as an intense rilvalry on the field a few years later when we would lock horns on opposite sides in state cricket. It is a delightful irony that 15 years later, Stuart Law and I would complete our Australian first class careers on the same day. In fact our paths would keep intertwining throughout that period.

We worked harder than I could have imagined was possible but we went out on Friday and Saturday nights to spend some of our $10 weekly allowance, usually to Ambassador's in the city, which was a cricketers' hang-out complete with a dance floor and music. I might have been well coordinated on the cricket field but I had a couple of left feet as a dancer.

My year at the academy was fruitful. Under the coaching of Jack Potter and his assistant Peter Spence, the academy opened my eyes to the professionalism you needed at that level; I reckon it is one of the reasons why other nations have been left behind by Australia at the top level.

We went on country tours playing games, and a couple of times we used the facilities at the AIS in Canberra. We met Sir Donald Bradman, who signed a book for all of us. We were exposed to sports science, new fitness techniques, sports psychology and a range of ways to improve our cricket.

My only criticism is that they did not have any specific coaching in wicketkeeping, for in the early days of the academy the idea of importing coaches for specialist areas was still being developed. But I came out of the academy in 1989 feeling like a better player.

* * *

At the end of that year I was planning on going home to Victoria. Michael Dimattina, a good keeper, was the gloveman for the Vics and seemed ensconced in the job after five years. I knew that I would be his understudy, but I would at least be in the state squad.

But Peter Anderson, South Australia's wicketkeeper in the Sheffield Shield competition at that time, changed all that for me. I was in awe of Anderson, whom I'd watched at Adelaide Oval throughout the previous season. We'd had a few catches together at practice and he was an inspiration to me.

Anderson kept like an Englishman, employing soft hands and the sharpest reflexes up to the stumps. He reminded me of Alan Knott and Bob Taylor, two English keepers who I had admired in the past. But he was a Queenslander by birth, and he was finding it difficult to secure employment in Adelaide. Anderson wanted to go home.

David Hookes, then South Australia's captain, approached me at the end of my time in the academy and told me about Anderson's situation. There were two other young keepers in the running for the job of replacing him, and there was the possibility that the selectors would go back to Wayne Phillips, who had kept in the past. But Hookes said I would have a chance if I stayed in Adelaide.

Now my heart was Victorian then and always will be. I'd never even thought about representing another state. But I spoke to Mum and Dad about it, and we agreed it was a case of: "Right place, right time." I went to Darwin playing cricket with some mates in the off-season and gave it some more thought. I knew that Hookes had plenty of power, even though I had not been given any guarantees. Ultimately I went with my head, rather than my heart, and made my home in Adelaide.

I moved into a house in the suburb of Hope Valley with Joe Scuderi, who had also opted to stay on rather than return to his native Queensland at the completion of his academy year. Scuderi's room was plastered with posters of the rock band Kiss, his passion of the time. Michael Bevan, a future Test batsman, moved in with us for a period, which was interesting to say the least.

Bevan had taken up a scholarship in the second intake of the academy and even then, had a reputation for tantrums. These were known in cricket circles as "Bev-Attacks". I will never forget the time a girlfriend of mine from Perth awoke our household with a late phone call, forgetting the time difference to Adelaide. I could hear Bevan screaming in his room and when he came out, I told him to shut up and relax. At that point he picked up a fork from the sink and threw it straight at me. The cutlery flew over my shoulder and embedded itself in the wall behind me, leaving four distinct holes in the plasterboard.

Of course there were no hard feelings and Bevan was fine the next day. But that was some temper he had!

I got through the trial games and played my first senior game for SA against Queensland in a one-dayer in Adelaide, then against Victoria the following day. I made my first class debut on November 3, 1989, against Queensland at Brisbane, my nerves jangling. Behind the confident façade was a trembling teenager who had managed to spill a cup of coffee in his lap on the flight up from Adelaide. I had to cover the stain with a jumper tied around my waist and face the television cameras that greeted us at the airport with some dignity intact.

It was an occasion memorable for the terror of facing Craig McDermott and Carl Rackemann for an hour-and-a-half for a measly 6 runs on a Gabba seamer. I can still see the big, blonde Rackemann launching balls that kept flying under my chin, and I can still hear the constant abuse of Greg Ritchie, Queensland's former Test batsman, who stood in the slips and sneered at my appearance: "Fucking academy boy! He won't last."

Now cricket is a hierarchical game in Australia and young blokes quickly discover that they take these lessons on board or they will perish. And until they have graduated, they keep their trap shut. It's a hard school, no doubt.

David Hookes was my initial first class captain and it is accurate to say that he barely spoke more than a word or two to me in the first three or four games of first class cricket that I played. Hookes stood at first slip alongside me when we were in the field, not more than two metres away from me for over-after-over, but there was none of the banter or chat that you would expect in that situation.

What this meant was that I had not graduated. Then a few games into the season I went horizontal to my left in front of

Hookes at slip to catch the New Zealander Mark Greatbatch in a tour game at Adelaide Oval. It was one of the best catches I ever took, an absolute blinder in the left glove, later described by Neil Hawke in the 'News' as "bordering between the spectacular and the miraculous". Rolling over on the turf and feeling chuffed with myself, I felt Hookes' hand ruffle the back of my head and he uttered something to the effect of: "Good catch, son."

And right then and there, I knew that I had made it to step one.

People might find this strange, but I understand perfectly what Hookes was doing. Firstly, you need to realise that he came from the Ian Chappell old school of cricket thinking, which instructs that a new player must show himself to be good enough to join his colleagues in the big time. Secondly, you need to remember that I was a Victorian, and Victorians don't get too many favours in Adelaide. It was Hookes' team, and I had to earn his respect.

I was learning on the job. South Australia had Tim May, the best off-spinner I ever saw and the toughest single bowler that I ever kept to because he was such a big turner of the ball, and so many balls went 'through the gate' on the batsman, always a tough delivery to take. We had Peter Sleep, the leg-spinner whom Hookes didn't believe could bowl at all. We had Darren Lehmann, the amazing young batsman whom I would room with for most of the season, and Colin 'Funky' Miller, another former Victorian.

And of course we had Hookes himself, a freak with the bat. I have a vivid memory of him turning the blade on its side in the Adelaide Oval nets one day when I was behind him, keeping to the spinners, and using the edge of the bat to smash Sleep back over his head. Not once, but quite a few times, too. Here was more of the Hookes I came to know, who could not accept the idea that Sleep was a decent bowler, despite the fact that 'Sounda' had played Test cricket for Australia. But I would defy anyone to hit a decent leg-spin bowler so far with the edge of his bat. It was incredible.

We made the final of the national one-day championship in Perth and got rolled for 87 batting first, so that Western Australia had parcelled up the title before they needed to turn on the WACA Ground lights. We were a middle-of-the-road third in the Sheffield Shield competition, although we had one memorable day at Adelaide Oval in January when Joe Scuderi's incredible 6/6, bowling gentle swingers on a perfect pitch, skittled Western Australia for 41 as I snared four catches behind the stumps.

I had a good year with the gloves with 34 dismissals in 12 matches and broke an obscure wicketkeeping world record that still stands. I didn't concede a bye for half a dozen games but I hadn't a clue until I was told by some local journalists partway through that season that there was a record for such things. The Englishman Keith Andrew, who played for Northamptonshire, had not conceded a bye during the scoring of 2132 runs by opposition teams in 1965.

It was this record I overtook at the MCG against Victoria in the middle of the season, but it almost never happened. During an earlier first class match against Sri Lanka at Adelaide Oval in December I top-edged a pull shot from Champaka Ramanayake into my nose, smashing it all over my face. When I went into the dressing rooms Tim May reeled away in horror at the sight and sound of our doctor straightening it, a process far more painful than the initial blow itself. The next day, I couldn't see out either eye and for a week, I had to wear this Hannibal Lecter-style facemask so that it would settle.

Someone had to take the gloves for Sri Lanka's second innings, and the multi-talented Hookes was the man. What I would soon learn was that my captain was not thrilled by the thought of the upstart keeper breaking a world record, a prospect that had made the newspapers.

Hookes tried to nobble me by deliberately dropping the third ball of Sri Lanka's innings, allowing the batsmen to run through for a bye. But when the journalists researched this, it emerged that my streak would stay intact since I was not actually keeping at the time. With hindsight, I know that my captain was putting me back in my place.

I didn't miss a game that season, which was a tough initiation to say the least. My world record run expired in Perth against Western Australia in an incredible match where Hookes inserted the Sandgropers and we conceded 0/283 on the dreadful first day. Geoff Marsh played and missed at Peter Gladigau's first, gentle outswinger of the day and I swear that scarcely another ball flew into my gloves for the remainder. Marsh made 355 and put on 431 with Mike Veletta, his opening partner. We didn't have the luxury of celebrating a wicket until Hookes himself broke through halfway through the second day, by which time we'd been annihilated.

My keeping record expired when Marsh tried to tickle a ball from Tim May and it ran from his thigh pad away to fine leg for a single. The umpire, Ric Evans, signalled 'byes' and I was furious. "Just fucking get on with it," said Hookes.

This was my introduction to Shield cricket.

There was a day at Adelaide Oval when, inexplicably, we had been rained off while an academy game at the adjacent No. 2 oval was continuing. Seeing this from the back of the stand, I chose to wander over in my shorts for a chat with some of the boys who had succeeded me at the AIS.

After half an hour the rain eased and I wandered back, passing the Western Australian coach, Daryl Foster in the nets. "Chuck, I don't want to alarm you, but we're on in five minutes," he said. I thought Foster was cranking me up. But I hurried up the stairs to the dressing room only to run into Hookes, fully kitted out, leading the South Australian team back on to the field for the resumption of play.

At this point I was wearing shorts and a shirt and no shoes and remember, for a moment, that I was the new kid in the team. Meticulous with my equipment, I always taped my fingers and would generally take 15 minutes to get ready. "I'd fucking hurry up if I was you," said the skipper.

Hookesy did not organise another keeper or take the 12th man on to the field with the team that day when I went missing. They waited on the ground for me until the crowd began to get restless. He was quite prepared to publicly humiliate me to teach me a lesson. I dropped the first four balls that came to me that day, but it needs to be said that I never repeated my mistake.

It was a hard year for lots of reasons, not least of which was Hookes' hardline attitude. But there is no doubt that he taught me plenty. I learned about mental toughness and I came out of the experience a harder person. Sooner than I could know, I would need to draw on those reserves.

CHAPTER 5 THE WEST INDIES

I was on a five-month sojourn to Darwin, playing cricket and working for a landscaping company as a glorified lawnmowing man, when I received a phone call that would turn my life upside down.

It was the winter of 1990 and a couple of mates had joined me at the Top End for a few games of cricket to fill the gap in time until the next Sheffield Shield season.

The call was to inform me that my father Roy was gravely ill back in Melbourne. Dad had been treated for cancer a couple of years earlier, but had recovered for a period. Now he was in trouble again, and I caught the first flight to Melbourne and drove to the hospital to be with him.

Dad was an elderly man by this stage and suffered emphysema from 50 years of smoking. I left Darwin on a Friday, and by the following Monday, I watched Dad take his last breath, standing in his hospital room while the rest of my family were having a coffee in the visitors' lounge. This was a horrible experience and one that would stay with me for some time.

His death knocked the stuffing out of me, especially since it seemed to have happened so quickly. I cancelled the rest of my

Darwin trip and stayed with Mum, who was virtually wheelchair-bound with a back problem by this time. It was also around this time that I began to think about coming back to Victoria to live and play my cricket.

But a few weeks after Dad's passing, I was picked in the Australian Under 21 team to make a tour of the West Indies in July-August, and I had no choice but to lift myself out of the malaise. Jamie Cox from Tasmania, my mate from the academy, was the captain, and Brendon Julian of Western Australia was his deputy. The team also included a couple of blokes with big reputations: the Western Australian batsman Damien Martyn, another close friend in fast bowler Damien Fleming, and a chap called Shane Warne of Victoria.

Now I knew Warnie, of course, but not well. We'd been at some under-age squad trainings together in Melbourne previously, and my very first memory of him is that one day he drove into the Junction Oval with the music blaring from his car like a mug lair. I would come to know him better on this tour, which included three Youth Tests at Barbados, Jamaica and Guyana plus an assortment of other matches throughout the islands of the Caribbean.

Initially the relationship between Warnie and I was one of spin bowler to keeper. It's a special union, that one, for it needs to be. But later on, Warnie and I nominated ourselves to sit on the so-called fines committee that every cricket tour seems to have, where team-members are singled out and made to pay for various indiscretions, and we bought pink hats and pink shorts as the committee uniform. We started to bond. We were both St Kilda supporters and similar in character, I suppose, so we had a bit in common. We would call Warnie 'Bloodnut' because of his red hair, or 'Coze', after the former Australian Test cricketer and redhead Gary Cosier, or 'Brunsie', after the Geelong footballer

Neville Bruns. He hated being teased about his hair colour and this was perhaps the start of his long affair with the blonde rinse. He actually dyed his entire melon blonde early in the trip to avoid our constant taunts about his orange-coloured hair. He struggled with the food on tour and he wrote an entry in my diary toward the end which reads: "I just want to go home and have a large Hawaiian pizza." We were all feeling our way with the world.

The first thing that struck me about Warnie as a bowler was that he could spin the ball miles. He had these thick fingers and strong hands and he could rip it like I'd never seen anyone rip it. But back then, he had no control over what he was bowling. I can remember chasing them down leg-side and catching them wide outside the off-stump as well, but he took seven wickets in an innings in a game against Leeward Islands at St Kitt's and it was a landmark trip for him. It was the tour when good judges began whispering about the kid from Victoria with the fizzing leg-spinner.

It was my first overseas trip of any sort and the cricket was a success. I scored 102 not out at the Test venue Sabina Park in Kingston, against the Jamaican under 21 team. We won the Test series comfortably, and I took over from the ailing Cox to skipper the team for the latter part of the third Test match in Guyana.

Even then, the signs of the steady demise of West Indian power in cricket were evident. Sherwin Campbell, their captain and best player, was the only one in that team to kick on in any significant way. They had no structure to their cricket and we were on the way up. You could sense it, even though it would not be until 1995 that Mark Taylor's Australian team would dethrone the mighty Caribbean champions at the top level.

But it was a test of our resilience in other ways. The accommodation we were given was often deplorable. In Guyana we were put up in the police barracks in 38-degree heat with no air conditioning but were thankful at least for mosquito nets to drape over ourselves. In Berbice, Guyana, we slept eight to a room in a guesthouse after a bus trip that opened all of our naïve, young eyes. There were people defacating at the riverside, then a few metres down, others washing their dishes, then a few metres down others bathing. We couldn't sleep at night because of the heat, so we sat up playing cards and dominoes.

The airline we used, BWIA, was quickly christened But Will It Arrive? Virtually every flight was delayed, and we would sit around airports in our team uniform in 35-degree heat sweltering, in one case for seven hours. We were a youth team and there was no special attention provided. No upmarket guest lounges for us.

These were times when we all realised how lucky we were to live in a country like Australia. I suppose it was a shock to most of us, because that image of the West Indies taken from the postcards was ingrained on us.

Kingston, the Jamaican capital, has the reputation as one of the world's most violent cities. We were told not go out at night unless we were in a group of at least six players, and advised that it would be best not to go out after dark at all. But we were kids. Four of us walked to Kentucky Fried Chicken one night and promptly found ourselves followed by a group of men. The security guard at the KFC – complete with hand gun – escorted us home and told us not to repeat the episode.

At one of our hotels, there were two young kids, about 13 or 14, begging us for money each day when we boarded the team bus. One day I brushed this kid and said: "I'm going to the cricket. I haven't got any money!" To which he started saying: "You give me money or I kill you. Give me money or I kill you!"

I didn't think that much of this but when we pulled back into the hotel that night in the bus, this kid was waiting. And this time, he was holding up a machete. "Give me money or I kill you," he was saying. The driver locked the bus and the security staff from the hotel shepherded us through. I didn't go out that night.

It's not exactly the picture-perfect West Indian image of the beaches and the palm trees. But yes, we did go to some beautiful places and we did play cricket on the sand and yes, the people were wonderful. They loved their cricket and there were good crowds at the matches. I can remember the gorgeous resort of Ocho Rios in Jamaica and we all loved Antigua, the island that is home to the great Sir Vivian Richards.

We spent a memorable afternoon at the Barbados home of Arthur 'Scobie' Breasley, the famous Australian jockey who had settled in the Caribbean. We met a few of the West Indian cricket greats, such as Michael Holding, and went to functions attended by Sir Garry Sobers, Wes Hall and the like, legends of the game.

At Bridgetown, the capital of Barbados, we found what might be my favourite night spot in the world, Harbour Lights, where the bar at the back stretched out on to the beach and the Calypso music belted out from inside.

It was at Harbour Lights at the end of the tour that I belted Damien Martyn, with repercussions that I cannot specify to this day. Now Marto and I had got on well on this tour, both of us having a confident side to our characters. I was rooming with Jamie Cox, but sometimes if we had to share a triple room, he would come and join us.

Maybe we were too similar. But the tension started to build when our competitive streaks came to the fore, especially out in the night club scene. It sounds ridiculous now, but Marto had this habit of cutting in if you were chatting to a girl and saying things like: "Have you told this bird you've got a baby on the way back home?" He thought it was funny and plainly I didn't, especially when it happened half a dozen times.

In St Kitt's, I roomed with him in this tall hotel building and one night I had no clean clothes to go out in. Cox had expended his wardrobe too, and Marto had already left. So I borrowed one of his shirts and wore it out. When Marto saw me, he cracked the shits. We'd nicknamed him 'Bam Bam', after the Flintstones character, by then, because if something went wrong, he was first to blow up.

I told him I'd get his shirt dry-cleaned and to chill out. But when I got back to the room, he had thrown my cricket 'coffin' out the hotel window and my gear was strewn all over the hotel grounds. Anyone who knows how meticulous I am about my gear will know how angry I was.

As I said, it's all laughable now. But back at Harbour Lights at the end of our trip, we were out enjoying ourselves and Marto was chatting to a girl at the bar. Me being the smart-arse, I took my revenge, waltzing up and saying something like: "Marto, does this girl know you're going back to Perth to get married?"

He pushed me away but his finger poked me in the eye, probably by accident. That's when I punched him in the face and split his lip wide open. He was crying and what upset me was that he went straight to the coach, Steve Bernard, and the manager, Brian Taber, who were in the bar and blurted out: "Look what Chuck's done to me!"

Taber came over and I apologised. But the reason I relate this story is that I have no doubt it left a black mark against me with officialdom for years afterward. I know for a fact that it was mentioned in the tour reports back to the Australian Cricket

Board, and my cards were marked, so to speak. With hindsight, I know it was a bad move. Marto was a smart-arse back then, and one of his Western Australian teammates told me he wished that he had landed the punch himself. But I was 19, and there'd been a build-up of tension. I just made a mistake.

It was a long tour for boys just out of home. A lot of us struggled with the food, living on chicken and rice. I was still dealing with the death of Dad and I had the distraction of deciding my future. Victoria was increasingly in pursuit of my services.

Early in that tour I heard that my mate Darren Lehmann was defecting to Victoria and I rang my old coach, Les Stillman, to get the lowdown. Stillman had crossed to the Vics as well. Victoria had suffered two seasons on the bottom of the Shield table, and the administration had opted to move away from the time-honoured policy of declining interstate imports. Fast bowler Alan Mullally, from Perth, was coming too.

Stillman told me that Lehmann was moving east and that the Victorians may want me as well. The wheels were in motion. A few days later he rang me to ask me if I would come back to Melbourne. Then Swan Richards, the head of the Gray Nicolls equipment company, rang to encourage me and so did John Scholes, the former Victorian player. Stillman rang and said he believed that I could beat Michael Dimattina and take the wicketkeeper's berth.

This was all very well. I wanted to go home to Victoria to be close to Mum. I'd formed a rapport with a girl called Katherine, the best friend of my niece (who was my age, by the way) from Cranbourne, a young woman who had comforted me when I was at my lowest after the death of Dad. There were good reasons to go back.

But I was a member of the South Australian team. Victoria was offering no such guarantees; in fact Dimattina had been the keeper for six years. So there was a risk involved for me. Needless to say, keepers don't get the luxury of two or three a side.

I talked to Jamie Cox about it and he asked me what my heart was telling me. When I said I wanted to play for Victoria, he said there was no issue. On 27 August in the nightmare of Berbice, no doubt on another hot and sleepless night, I wrote in my diary: "I've decided tonight to return to my home state, Victoria."

CHAPTER 6 HOME TO THE BIG 'V'

I'd like to say it was an easy homecoming to my native state, but that wouldn't be strictly true. At least not initially.

It was the old wicketkeeper's lament. I'd been brought into the squad by Les Stillman, the state coach, but the incumbent keeper was Michael Dimattina. He was a good keeper too, only 25 years old, and a player I respected, a guy who'd been in the job for six years. Now we were head-to-head for the one and only position available.

Worse, Dimma was close to Merv Hughes and Tony Dodemaide and some of the heavies of the team. It made for an uncomfortable environment for me when I joined state squad training in Melbourne after the Caribbean tour. I'd been given no guarantees by Stillman or Bill Lawry, the Test legend who had been made cricket manager for Victoria in the wake of consecutive bottom-place finishes. But with hindsight, I can see that Dimattina's cards had been marked after Victoria's two bad seasons on the trot. Years down the track I'd experience the same feeling, and that's just a fact of life for a keeper. I never spoke to him about it, but I know that he was shattered when the selectors chose me ahead of him.

On the one hand I was pumped up to have the chance of playing for Victoria. But I was still a kid, and I didn't know Hughes or Dodemaide or Dean Jones or Simon O'Donnell, the captain. Damien Fleming and Shane Warne were my mates in the squad and we stuck together, along with Darren Lehmann, who had made the move across the border from Adelaide.

Hughes, Dodemaide and Jamie Siddons were all good mates and they were forced to accept me despite their reservations about the removal of Dimattina. They never rejected me or made me feel uncomfortable. But one thing stands out to me, especially about Hughes and Dodemaide. They influenced me in the way that they trained and they instilled in me the meaning of what it meant to play for Victoria. They regarded it as a huge honour and they took the attitude that whether they were playing for their club Footscray, for Victoria or Australia, they played with the same intensity. The level of competition made no difference to them, and I will never forget that.

Back then, the Victorian dressing room had an awkward feel for me. O'Donnell was an old-school-style captain, and he ruled by creating fear of his leadership. He didn't want to hear other people's opinions, he was abrasive, and he wanted everyone to know that he was in charge.

There was a division between the older players and the newer guys and just as I'd experienced in South Australia the previous year under Hookes (who, incidentally, had been sacked by the South Australian Cricket Association and replaced by Andrew Hilditch), I had to earn my stripes as the new boy. It would be fair to say I had my teething problems with O'Donnell, who once or twice went through the crease in the nets to bowl bouncers at me. Or perhaps those personal difficulties might go back to that first year when he humiliated me over my batting.

O'Donnell would read out the batting order before a match and he'd gradually shuffle me down the list in a theatrical way. It went like this: "No. 7 is Chuck … oh hang on, No. 7 is Doddy, No. 8 is Chuck!" Once in Perth that season they would bat me at 11, but O'Donnell started reading out my name at seven, and slid me down, one slot at a time, to last. In the end it took Merv Hughes' intervention – "Ease up will ya" – to stop the skipper from deliberately humiliating me any more.

That's the way things were back then. There were the senior guys and the rookies and ne'er the twain shall meet, so to speak. Flem and I were hardly game enough to move sometimes. I have this vivid memory of one of the senior men, with his feet up on the esky in the rooms one day having a cigarette. "Hey Flemo," he says. "Get me a beer!" Flem was 12th man that day. "Flem don't have a shower yet. Keep your whites on until we have our shower."

It wasn't a unified situation and it was a problem of Victorian cricket when I was younger. And it is the reason why years after this, when I became a leader of the team, I went out of my way to make the younger blokes feel like we were one unit and that they were part of it. But back when I started, the attitude was: "We've played this much, so back off!"

Don't get me wrong, here. It wasn't all bad. We had a good time socially that year, and a lot of that goes to 'Scuba' O'Donnell's credit. When we came home from Shield trips interstate we'd get the wives and girlfriends and go to the Eldorado Hotel in North Melbourne. Scuba would be half-cut and he'd be up the front singing 'Billy, Don't Be A Hero' and he'd get everyone up there with him for the sing-song.

Sometimes he was away with the Australian one-day international team. Siddons captained the team when he was away, and I loved playing under him. O'Donnell was a defensive captain but Siddons would attack; he'd back his side. And we had quite a team.

Back in 1990 state cricket had not turned professional and I had a job in marketing at the State Bank which had been organised by Geoff Parker. It was so not me, but I was thankful of the chance to earn some money, as there were no state contracts back then. It would be nearly a decade before the formation of the players' union and resulting better conditions for state players. But I didn't care back then. Mum had moved to Cranbourne from Wonthaggi and was living in a flat at the rear of my sister's home there, so I could keep in touch with her. I was going out with Kath. And I was living my dream, playing for Victoria and hoping to play for Australia, though the Queenslander Ian Healy had taken a hold on the keeper's position in the Test team.

I made my debut under the navy blue cap of Victoria against Queensland at the Gabba that season. I remember that Paul Reiffel was fuming because he'd been made 12th man despite the Gabba's reputation for being seamer-friendly, and Allan Mullally, the import, was in the side. Not only that, but Stillman and O'Donnell had taken the leg-spinner Peter McIntyre into the game on a wicket that was more than a tinge green.

'Pistol' was filthy. He brought the drinks out at one stage and, being young and stupid, I casually asked him: "Is there any water?" Pistol, who is the mildest of men, threw the drink bottle toward me and said: "What's that? A fucking block of flats?"

It is a matter of record that the laconic Paul Reiffel would finish the season with 49 first class wickets, the best performance by a Victorian in 20 years, having begun the year carrying the drinks.

That season was the first time I got to know Jones, the legendary Test and one-day international batsman who took me under his wing. We roomed together and would do so for the next four years. I respected him as a magnificent player. He called me 'Young Punk' all the time and he'd say: "Stick with me, champ". We were close, which is the reason why a few years later when we fell out, it hurt me all the more.

At full strength we had a superb cricket team, what with the world class batting of Jones, Lehmann and Siddons and the pace bowling attack headed by Hughes, Dodemaide, Reiffel and Fleming, plus some excellent players around the edges including a sometime Test all-rounder in O'Donnell, the skipper. At that point I thought Fleming, my Youth teammate and friend, would play 100 Tests for Australia. He swung the ball prodigiously, he had the best slower ball around, and he had the knack of finding ways to get wickets. Siddons was an absolute freak, one of the finest batsmen I've seen and an amazing fieldsman as well. Out of all the players I walked out with over 15 years, it stuns me most to think that Siddons never played a Test match for his country. But in the ensuing years most of that group would spend considerable time under the baggy green cap of Australia in Test cricket. We had a hell of a team.

Of course we lost that first-up game in Queensland, skittled by Craig McDermott and Carl Rackemann, a ritual for Victorians on the Gabba greentop. But we wound our way into the season, beating New South Wales by an innings in Melbourne behind Siddons' unbeaten 245. In Hobart I came close to my first century, getting 98 against Tasmania, caught down the leg-side trying to hook Rod Tucker after we were in trouble on the first day, but we played a dull draw. I will always remember batting with Merv Hughes during that game. When Tasmania employed a leg-slip for Merv, he walked down the wicket to me and said: "What a waste of time that is. No one ever gets caught at leg slip." A few balls later, sure enough, the big fella was on his way back to the pavilion, caught at leg-slip. It was the one and only time in my career I couldn't stop laughing at the dismissal of one of my teammates.

Siddons smashed another double-century against South Australia in Adelaide and we were within millimetres of winning by an innings, but had to be content with a draw, SA holding out at nine-wickets-down in the second dig. The turning point came in Perth where Merv Hughes' second-innings 6/54 took us to an outright win, our first at the WACA for 10 years. Hughes was rapt, walking around the dressing room and holding up his beer and saying: "TFY, fellas." We had no idea what he was talking about until he explained: "Ten fucking years." My six catches equalled the state record for an innings.

In February there was a portent of things to come when O'Donnell blew up in public at the Victorian Cricket Association over practice facilities after we suffered a bad defeat in Sydney. O'Donnell was chastised by the administration over his comments and the tension remained. It was also the season that Shane Warne debuted in first class cricket, copping a hammering against Western Australia and taking 1/102 at the Junction Oval. Little did we know that superstardom was just around the corner for him, for he mostly sat behind Paul Jackson in the spinners' stakes that season.

But by the time we reached the last match against Queensland, at St Kilda's Junction Oval, there were various possibilities. Dodemaide, who'd been in and out of the side owing to our overstock of fast bowlers, stepped up here. Set 193 to win in the fourth-innings and host the Shield final, Dodemaide ripped through the Queenslanders with 5/19, flattening them for only 79. During that match, I overtook Ian Maddocks' state record for wicketkeeper's dismissals, his 43 set in the 1977-78 season. More importantly, the victory secured the home final for Victoria and we were going to the MCG, where we hadn't played all season because of the construction of the Great Southern Stand.

Victoria had not won the great, big trophy carved in Lord Sheffield's honor for 11 years, and our opponent would be the fiercest of our rivals, New South Wales, winner of nearly twice as many national titles as any other state. But with hindsight, it's possible to say we were destined to win this one. Australia's Test team under Allan Border was touring the Caribbean and trying to unseat the world champion West Indians led by Viv Richards, and New South Wales had provided five players for that squad. Victoria had to make do without Dean Jones and Merv Hughes, significant losses. But the Blues were missing Steve and Mark Waugh, Peter Taylor, Mike Whitney and Greg Matthews, almost half their team.

It was an amazing game when at the end of each day, a different winner looked likely. Fleming's four wickets helped us to knock over the Blues for 223 in the first innings but we replied with only 119, my unbeaten 25 being second-top score. Enter AIC Dodemaide, the Footscray seamer who taught me that year how to play as a professional, day in-day out. Dodemaide took 5/25 to get us back into the game, and New South Wales extracted only 134 on a true pitch. Midway through the fourth day we set out in pursuit of 239 to win the match and the Shield but the tension was unrelenting. "The hardest game of cricket I've ever played in," O'Donnell would call it later, noting that at least the 1987 World Cup final in the cauldron of Calcutta's Eden Gardens, in which he played, was all over in a day.

A double-century stand from Wayne Phillips (91 not out) and Siddons (124 not out) did the trick for us when Phillips nudged a ball behind square at 4.44 on the final day, giving us an eight-wicket win. Siddons had been magnificent, passing 1000 runs for the season for the second year in a row, belting 15 boundaries and one six off Michael Bevan that soared into the construction site. Phillips the quiet man was brilliantly efficient at the other end, telling Siddons to get on with the job when the latter offered to farm the strike for him late in the chase so that he, too, could extract a century. "I said: 'No. Just keep going for it'," said Phillips.

I'll never forget the pride in my heart when Simon O'Donnell lifted that enormous shield, nor the celebrations at the Toc H nightclub that night, for we knew how to enjoy our wins. Fleming and myself were virtually babies at the game and we'd already tasted big-time success, my 48 catches for the season breaking a Victorian record, and Flem being earmarked for international cricket with that picture-perfect outswinger. Looking back, that victory must have been pre-determined, because New South Wales were decimated by their absences and their second team wasn't all that strong. We'd been lucky that Dodemaide had run through Queensland that fateful day at the Junction, and that the Bulls had taken the gas yet again, and even then it took an astonishing partnership between Siddons and Phillips to get us over the line. "Vics finally do it," read *The Age* headline. 'VICS BOLT IN' said the *Herald Sun*. It was a triumph that had been too long coming for our state.

As the Sheffield Shield holder, we were entitled to a trip to England to play against the county champions of 1991, Essex. Unfortunately there was a stink before we even made the tour in September. Opening batsman Gary Watts had retired after the Shield final but we'd all been told that the winning team would make the trip to England and we felt Watts should go. Dean Jones and Merv Hughes, whose absence from the final was due to their international duties, were added to the squad but Watts was not selected. Instead, the VCA added Darrin Ramshaw, a batsman from Western Australia whom they had attracted to Melbourne for the 1991-92 season. Watts was dirty but Ramshaw made the trip as part of a 14-man squad.

We played a match at Durham in the north of England and then a one-dayer and a first class match against Essex, the county which boasted Graham Gooch and Neil Foster to name a couple. In the first class game at Chelmsford, we were saved from defeat by rain on the final day. But they were heady times for a kid from Wonthaggi. Our fitness adviser, Mark 'Muddy' Waters, (Now the Davis Cup Tennis fitness advisor) took us for a training run through the streets of London to Hyde Park for a kick of the footy, and people turned their heads to see the likes of Hughes and Jones, household names in that part of the world.

Cricket takes you to some amazing places. I roomed with Jones again and one day in London I answered the phone in our hotel and it was for Deano. When I asked who was calling, the reply I got was: "Tell him it's EJ." Now I thought about this for a moment and I knew that Jonesy had a contract with the Adidas company for his footwear, and I also knew that Ted 'EJ' Whitten, the legendary former Footscray footballer, was the Adidas man in Melbourne. Straight away I said to Jones: "Teddy's on the phone." So Jonesy takes the call and when he hangs up, he looks at me and says: "You idiot. That was Elton John! He wants us to come around for a beer!"

Remember, here, that I'm just out of my teens, making my first senior overseas tour, and I'm rooming with an experienced guy. Of course I thought Jones was winding me up about the invitation from one of the entertainment industry's superstars. Half an hour later I'm in a big black cab with Jones, Merv Hughes and Damien Fleming, who was rooming with Merv, and we're heading off to Elton John's place. We pull up at what looks to be an unpretentious, single-front terrace, and Elton's butler opens the door. The house went forever, it had an in-ground pool with a dance floor over the top of it. It had the lot.

So we sit in Elton John's lounge room and he gives us a beer and we chat about cricket and other things, and the kid from Wonthaggi is wondering how in hell an international music superstar knows so much about cricket; knows that Victoria has won the Sheffield Shield, knows that I'm the wicketkeeper and asks me a few questions about the art. And I'm looking at my mate Flem and we're probably thinking the same thing about this surreal moment.

"How good's this?"

Backyard Test Match '70s style. Me posing for the camera early in my career.

Dad's (front row, second from right) World War II HMAS Vampire cricket team.

East Wonthaggi under-16s, 1981. I'm with my most prized possession, my red wicket keepers gloves. My first coach, Colin Bolding is standing in the middle of the back row.

George Murray – the person responsible for giving me the opportunity to play 1st XI cricket at Fitzroy/Doncaster Cricket Club.

With Mum and Dad in Adelaide in 1988.

*Me and Mum,
the early years.*

*Mum during her visit to the UK in 1993. She spent the last few years
of her life in a wheelchair due to chronic arthritis in her back.*

My two close friends from the bush. Steve McNamara (left) – my coach at Outtrim Moyarra Kongwak Cricket Club and Dennis Vague (right) – my year 12 co-ordinator at Wonthaggi High School.

Guy Freene, long time friend and funniest drunk I've ever seen.

A Wonthaggi boy through and through, my good friend Michael Scott.

The Fashion Police. Warney and I thought we looked good at the time in our fines committee outfits in the West Indies, 1990.

reputation preceded him as well. It was the best against the best, and it was fascinating. Tendulkar ran down the wicket and smashed Warne over cover; kept charging him no matter how much dip and swerve and spin our man could muster. If Warne beats you in flight, you are generally gone. But on this day, Tendulkar would just continue with his shot even when he was 'done' in the air. When he played straight, his bat looked a couple of centimetres wider than it ought to have been. I kept thinking: "I'm going to stump this bloke." But he'd just hit it further. He got 59 and I can't recall seeing a better 59. For the record I did stump him, though, giving me a line in the paper that was worth hanging on to: "Tendulkar std Berry b Warne 59."

* * *

I first met Andy Towle in the Bull Ring bar area under the MCG members' stand during the World Cup of 1992. Towle was captain of Macclesfield, a club in Cheshire in England, and I was interested in furthering my career with a stint overseas. His club wanted a professional player to bolster its stocks. We struck up a friendship quickly and kept in touch. A few months later our mutual requirements came together when a deal was done for me to play league cricket alongside him in England during the winter of 1992.

Macclesfield is a leafy area about 20 minutes south of Manchester, populated by a lot of rich soccer players and the well-heeled. I had no idea what I was walking into. Towle picked me up at the airport and we drove up to his house. The double-gates opened and I thought he was taking the piss. It was like a palace. "This is where I live," he said. Towle's family ran a paper merchant business and weren't short of a quid, to say the least.

Macclesfield competed in the Cheshire County league, which was slightly lower in standard than the famous Lancashire league nearby. There were some good players, a few guys who came from the Lancashire county team, and it was a decent standard without being exceptional. We played on Saturdays and during the week there was always a 'friendly' game on somewhere. You never struggled for somewhere to play cricket.

At this level of cricket in England, it's important to understand that the social side of the game is uppermost in importance. The grounds are delightful and the afternoon teas are to die for. It's a great way to play cricket but it's also one of the reasons why English cricket has struggled in recent years. It's not overly competitive, whereas in Australia, you would find guys going at each other wherever you watched a game of cricket.

Macclesfield hadn't won anything for ages, and when I turned up, I set about making an impact. Towle was captain but graciously gave me my head. He wanted some of the Australian mentality instilled, and I told them they had to practise. "Oh no, training? Let's go to pub!" they would say. I told them that if I was playing then we'd all train twice a week. There were guys in the first eleven who did not know the basics of catching a cricket ball. I just told them that I didn't play for fun, ruffling a few feathers.

Towle looked after my airfares, got me a car and covered all my expenses for the season but the benefits, of course, were mutual. I'd gone there specifically to work on my batting, which had already become a problem in some people's eyes at home. I got 1298 runs, a league record, with four centuries. I learned a little more about patience and waiting for the right ball to hit. This had been my downfall as a batsman and I knew it. But at Macclesfield, I was the opening batsman and I was expected to score most of the runs. Often it would be on a damp track against nagging seamers who would not give you any pace to work with, especially by comparison with first class bowlers.

Moreover Macclesfield won the "double", taking the league championship and the cup, and I came home to Australia with a renewed sense of my ability to bat, and ready to confront the new season.

* * *

Hindsight again tells me that things started to go awry for Victoria in 1992-93. We were last in the Sheffield Shield competition and runner-up in the one-dayers. Under O'Donnell's conservative captaincy, we did not win a single Shield game outright, and we had eight draws.

I began the District cricket season in October with my first century at that level, 104 not out against Essendon, and began to think I may have turned a corner with the bat. But my first class season would not reflect my confidence; I averaged just under 17 and had 35 dismissals. Despite having a good year at club level with my batting, I can recall speculation mounting about its effectiveness, and people questioning whether the need to change keepers, replacing Michael Dimattina, had necessarily been worthwhile.

Otherwise the season was memorable for a controversial drawn match against Tasmania at the MCG when I caught Rod Tucker high to my left at full stretch in a dive. Pushing myself up from the turf to join the celebrations, I accidentally left the ball on the ground, and Tucker stood there waiting for a decision from the umpire. The Tasmanians thought I had spilled the catch and their coach, Greg Shipperd, questioned me in the press, an irony since we would end up working closely together many years later.

We were hammered by New South Wales in the one-day final behind Michael Bevan's 64 not out, but my best memory is of a young left-hander named Adam Gilchrist walking out to bat and looking distinctly nervous. It was a close, tense game at that point and I could not resist the urge to give him a Victorian welcome. "We're not sure you're up to this level," I told him. Again we can laugh at the irony now.

During this period we introduced a team-bonding exercise we called 'Dead Ants', which attracted some publicity. A designated player had to make the 'Dead Ants' call over a 24-hour period, and everyone had to be there. When the call was made, you had to lay on your back with arms and legs in the air like a dead ant. And it didn't matter where you were at the time. We did it in airports while we were waiting for luggage; we did it in a flash restaurant in Perth once to the amusement or distraction of the other patrons. It was meant to be done away from the field of battle, but one day our coach Les Stillman called it as we walked off Adelaide Oval and the press began talking about it. Bill Lawry, the VCA's cricket manager, soon put a stop to it.

Some team-bonding was necessary, because disenchantment about the management of the team was beginning to build. Les Stillman was unpopular among the players, and O'Donnell was on his last legs as captain. At this time there was a saying among the team that you were "on the barbecue" if something went wrong. If someone was dropped from the side, he was "on the barbecue". We'd blow on our shoulder for effect, as if you were tending to the flames.

Hughes was the leader in this regard, and a story of a day at Dean Jones' home at Romsey, outside Melbourne, typifies how Merv used to operate. A few of us had gathered at Deano's for the naming of his daughter, Phoebe. The background to all this was that Kath had been less than thrilled at the idea of me going to

England for six months of cricket, leaving her to the Melbourne winter. With the formalities about to begin, a couple of fire engines turned up in the driveway and the local firemen raced in. They pointed the fire hoses at Kath, severely embarrassing her. "Are you the one who's on fire? We need to put these flames out!" they said.

Merv had orchestrated the whole thing. It had been a quiet day at the Romsey fire station.

* * *

I returned to England for the winter of 1993 to play with Macclesfield. The friendships I had made the previous year were strong and the chance to play all year round was too difficult to turn down.

It was an Ashes tour year and Ian Healy and Tim Zoehrer were on the job with the gloves for Australia as Allan Border's team pumped England again. I figured it wouldn't hurt to be around in case of an injury or mishap, and I'd enjoyed my first year at the club. This time I extracted 1102 runs and we won the double again. In one game against Poynton I declared to Towle that I was going to make a double-century, which had never been done in the league. I carved them for 196 not out, a league record, by the time the overs had expired.

It was a season in which I played two matches for Rest of the World teams, one against England at Jesmond at Dean Jones' invitation, and the other against Zimbabwe at Scarborough. The first one was a highlight, with Mum coming over to watch and a bowling attack boasting Courtney Walsh, Danny Morrison, Malcolm Marshall and Allan Donald, who was frighteningly quick. Gordon Greenidge and Viv Richards, the great West Indians, also were in the side. The boys from Macclesfield took the bus up to Jesmond for the day and plastered up signs reading: "Berry is a Macc lad." I was having a ball.

Those two winters in England left me with friendships that will last forever. Towle, the skipper, was one of two in my wedding party a few years later. It was a wonderful cricket experience, too, with the challenging conditions. Above all else I had fun, travelling down to the West Country to Devon and Cornwall to play mid-week games with the Cheshire Cats, a band of amateur players whose number included brain surgeons and a leg spinning Catholic priest by the name of Father Dave McGarry from Didsbury who I'll never forget because of his warm-up techniques and his serious attitude to the game. Upon taking a wicket, he would gather us all in and say: "Concentrate now lads, fresh batter."

The Cheshire county league banned overseas first class players at the end of that season, making a longer stay impossible. But I would go back later, much later.

* * *

Dean Jones was installed as captain of Victoria by the time the 1993/94 first class season began in Australia. Simon O'Donnell had faded away into retirement, and I was happy with the change. O'Donnell had taken us to too many draws, whereas Jones was willing to attack, which suited my style. It was his second stint in the job, having trodden on too many toes the first time a few years earlier.

It was a much more eventful season. Darren Lehmann went home to Adelaide, but we had found two fine, young batsmen in Matthew Elliott, who arrived as a big-time player with 175 not out in a chase for 278 against Western Australia at the MCG, and Brad Hodge, whose first season yielded 991 runs. Jones was

Jones, peeling off four centuries and averaging 76 for Victoria despite the continuing unwillingness of the national selectors to recall him to the Test side.

We finished fifth in both the Shield and one-day competitions, and I had 43 dismissals behind the stumps. A welcome surprise was my selection in the Prime Minister's XI match against the touring South Africans, and my elevation to an Australian XI which played against India in three one-day matches following the season.

We contended for the Shield final but a couple of things went against us. One was a fabulous game in Sydney against a full-strength New South Wales before Christmas when we were within a wicket of beating the team regarded as the best domestic cricket side on the planet (or at least that was what they used to say). The Blues were 9/275, chasing 306, with the renowned batting "rabbit" Glenn McGrath walking through the gate to bat when the umpires called it off because of bad light. We were all furious, especially Shane Warne, who'd bowled 40 overs and taken 5/77 and soon ploughed into the New South Wales dressing rooms to give them a spray of invective about attacking cricket.

In February, the selectors came up with one of the most amazing choices I can recall, plucking off-spinner Steve McCooke from Melbourne to play against Tasmania and Queensland. Completing the fairytale, McCooke took 6/35 to win the game for us against the Queenslanders at the MCG. I had three stumpings from him in one innings, a career-high. In the next game in Perth he played when he shouldn't have, he didn't bowl a ball and got a pair with the bat, never to play again. Both teams needed a result and we could scarcely find the pitch from the outfield. Not surprisingly, 20 wickets fell on the first day, the game was finished before lunch on the third day, and our bid for the final had been scuttled.

By the end of that season Deano was well and truly running his own show. The Victorian team was being filled up with players from his club, Melbourne, or at least that was the impression some of the other team-members had. This made the District final, between my own Fitzroy-Doncaster and Melbourne, all the more sweet. Our coach, John Scholes, called Melbourne the 'cravat-wearers' and us the 'fish and chip eaters' and needless to say, he hated Melbourne. Leigh Watts and Brendan Joyce duly put on a big stand to win the final for us.

As for Victoria, we had certainly changed the way we were playing under Jones. We had found some young players in Elliott and Hodge, plus the pace bowler Simon Cook and leg-spinner Craig Howard. By the end of that season, I felt like big-time success was not too far away again.

* * *

Queensland broke one of the most famous droughts in sporting history in the summer of 1994-95, but for Victoria it was a middling season. The Bulls won the Sheffield Shield to raucous celebrations at the Gabba, ending one of the longest hoodoos in sport and prompting newspaper headlines around the cricket-playing world.

Victoria contended for a time but ultimately finished third in the Shield, the only highlight being our first title of any sort in four years when we defeated South Australia in the final of the national one-day competition. It was a season memorable for the failed marketing decision by Victoria to wear shorts in the limited-overs competition, an experiment which did not last for long. I was the only player who refused, because as wicketkeeper I couldn't be expected to dive around in a pair of shorts.

Matthew Elliott made three centuries for the season but the big star was Jones, who launched an amazing assault on South Australian in Melbourne that would take him to 324 not out from 553 minutes with 28 fours and two sixes. We were on the other end of the stick against Queensland early in the season when Matthew Hayden's incredible 201 not out from just 239 balls against a bowling attack headed by Hughes, Reiffel and Simon Cook carried his team to a winning chase of 344.

We knocked over South Australia for 169 in the final of the Mercantile Mutual Cup and I was at the wicket with Elliott when we overtook the South Australians to win the limited-overs title. At first class level I had 45 dismissals for the season and averaged 21.50 with the bat. Toward the end of the season Jones announced that he was retiring from international cricket, drawing a big crowd to his tribute game at the MCG. The national selectors had made it plain they no longer wanted him. But having said his farewells, Jones, who was still a superb player, promptly made it clear that he would in fact turn out for his country if he was required.

At state level we were suffering for the scattergun selection policy under which players never felt they were safe. Guys like Warren Ayres, Rohan Larkin and Geoff Allardice all felt like they had a single game in which to prove themselves. In one season we used 26 players; more than two full teams. But to me, the selectors were trying to find the new sensation when the likes of Ayres, Larkin and Allardice had made truckloads of runs in club cricket and were all worthy batsmen. Jones felt that District cricket was rubbish, and that you couldn't make judgments about players from that level of cricket. But this was before the second

XI concept took off, and it was all those guys had to make a case for themselves.

Overall, though, I felt like we were close to something good. But we had spent four years underachieving, considering the players we had at our disposal. We had never quite gelled as a unit, yet the names in our team were world class. I was young and I didn't fully understand it. Reflecting back now, I know that we were not a unit. By the time the next season came around, we would disintegrate.

CHAPTER 8 POLITICS IN SPORT

The ugliest season of my cricketing life began with a piece of personal tragedy. In August, 1995, with Victoria in the middle of its pre-season campaign, my mother Norma fell ill and was diagnosed with cancer. With my father's death, the family had the benefit of some warning. But Mum went into hospital and passed away just a few weeks later, on September 9, a terrible shock to all of us.

I'd always been extremely close to Mum, perhaps because I was the last-born child, and the only one at home for much of the time after my siblings moved away. I was devastated by her death, on top of Dad's, but I responded in the only way I knew how. I privately dedicated the 1995-96 season to my parents. I decided I was going to play for Australia, and sooner rather than later.

It all began well. I hit the ball beautifully in the opening Sheffield Shield match at the Gabba in Brisbane, extracting 74 against a high quality bowling attack, knocking Craig McDermott back over his head for six. Not long after that in a tour match against Pakistan at the MCG, I broke the state record by collecting 11 catches in a match, reaching the landmark with a big, right-handed pluck in front of slip to get rid of Saqlain

Mushtaq from Brad Williams' bowling. It passed the previous record of 10, set by the legendary Ray 'Slug' Jordon in a Shield match against South Australia 25 years earlier. "I could hear Slug's voice in my head all the time, and I wanted to beat it, not just equal it," I told the press.

But we had made a poor start to the season as a team, losing to New South Wales at home, and it went pear-shaped on the trip to Adelaide to play South Australia. During SA's second innings, I hurt my back diving for a ball down the leg-side, and I could barely get to my feet, let alone continue. I had to leave the field.

Skipper Dean Jones took the gloves and soon enough snared a catch behind the stumps, theatrically waving to the rooms, where I was lying in a lot of discomfort, as though to say: "This is easy!" But a couple of overs later, he let a few byes through, and he ended up giving the job to youngster Clinton Peake.

Jones and I had fallen out somewhat on the pre-season trip to Darwin. For five years prior, we had roomed together and become good friends, closer than what many people realised. Deano had been good to me around the time of Mum's death. He was the first cricket person that I phoned with my sad news, and immediately he offered his support, going as far as offering financial assistance with the funeral if we needed it.

In Darwin, Deano had blown up because the 'fines committee' had caught him out on something or other, the penalty being to carry all our bags to the team bus. The fines system is common practice on many sporting team trips. Most players dislike the punishment but always agree as part of the team environment. The skipper initially refused his medicine; he didn't believe he should be required to fit in with the shenanigans, eventually much to the boys' amusement he agreed. When I got stuck into him later, he proceeded to tell me that he was humiliated, and that he wouldn't take stick "from any two-bit first class cricketer", a statement that cut me deeply. Soon after that, I asked Les Stillman, our coach, if I could room with someone else.

Jones had been dumped from the Australian Test team in the summer of 1992-93 and subsequently from the one-day team as well. No doubt he was still feeling the pinch. But Deano lost the plot in the summer of 1995-96 with ramifications for all of us. The tension was there from the start, and we lost dreadfully in Adelaide, falling apart on the final day. Jones came into the rooms and called the rest of us "spineless". At the usual post-match press conference outside the dressing rooms, he made a provocative statement to the media: "We need batting, a spinner and an all-rounder," he said. It doesn't sound like much all these years later, but there was a selection committee to decide such matters. It was insulting to the all-rounder Jason Bakker, spinner Craig Howard and probably to Rohan Larkin, a top-order batsman who had struggled in that game. Deano was starting to talk like a dictator. It had become "I need this" or "I need that" all the time, and the players were getting tired of the way he treated us.

None of the players initially heard this press conference but as we gathered in the Golden Wing Lounge at Adelaide airport that night, already annoyed at the defeat (and in my case, concerned about the prolapsed disc in my back), Jones' head popped up on the television news, and the quote about his needs for different players was aired. Players were shaking their heads in disbelief. I was annoyed. "That shut everyone up," said Jones, walking away from the group.

There wasn't one player in that Victorian team who did not respect Jones as a player, and the way he prepared himself to play cricket. He was in another league to most of us. What we didn't like was the way he treated people. He treated us like second-rate citizens sometimes. The younger guys in the group were in awe of him and I guess they just went along with it. But the more senior guys like Damien Fleming, Matthew Elliott and me had had enough. Jones thought he was a great leader of people, but the truth is that he alienated the players and turned them against him. When he was challenged, he wanted to bring in young kids who would follow him, rather than question him.

This is where I became caught in the middle of what became a furore, a story that hit the back pages of the Melbourne newspapers and a dispute that lasted for months. When Jones stormed off at the airport, a couple of us approached coach Les Stillman. "What's that about?" we said. "How can he treat people like that? They're shattered."

Stillman didn't disagree. He said something like: "When we get back to Melbourne, we'll have a meeting, just the players who were here. We'll talk about it, because it's not the team harmony that we want." We assumed that Stillman would take control from there. Stupidly, we thought he would pull the captain into line. But it never happened that way.

We held our meeting in the old dressing rooms under the grandstand at the Junction Oval in St Kilda, our home base, a couple of days later. There was plenty of tension in the air, understandably. Jones was up the front with his arms folded, clearly filthy. Stillman was there with him, at least to start with. "Boys, we've had a bad loss and things weren't great," said the coach. "It's over to you."

With that, Stillman walked to the back of the room and there was this terrible silence. "Who wants to start?" barked Jones, cutting the air with his words. "Who's got the problem?" The silence must have lasted for 30 seconds. I felt that Stillman had hung us out to dry. I'd assumed that he would run the meeting, form some sort of bridge between the players and the captain.

He'd obviously told Jones there were some complaints about his manner, but that was about it.

Eventually I said to Jones: "Look, Deano, we still want you as our captain. You're our best player. But you're treating us like shit." Others spoke up. Larkin and Bakker and Howard all spoke along similar lines. Warren Ayres spoke as well. Jones was defensive and angry. It was a nasty meeting. Aside from his introduction, Stillman said nothing.

When we played Tasmania in the next game, I was unavailable because of my injury. But Bakker, Larkin and Howard were omitted. Anyone who spoke up against Jones had gone. Hawthorn's Peter Roach, a 20-year-old AIS scholarship-holder, took my place in the team and scored a half-century. Meanwhile I was having twice-a-day physiotherapy and swimming at 5.30am to get myself right, aiming for the Christmas-New Year game against Western Australia in Perth. Late in December, I had a fitness test with Stillman at the Junction Oval. The coach was hitting catches to me as hard as he could from only a couple of metres away. A genius wouldn't have caught them. "Your back's okay, but I think you've lost a bit of touch," he said.

There had been rumours around town that the selectors wanted to continue with Roach. At the moment Stillman made that statement, I knew that I was in trouble. I could smell it. I sprayed the coach. "How am I supposed to catch them?" I said.

"You used to catch them," he said.

On Christmas Eve, 1995, the phone rang at home. It was Deano. "It's one of the hardest decisions I've ever had to make, mate. You've been left out for Perth." I guess I shouldn't have been so shocked. I'd seen it coming. Deano had been telling people around the cricket fraternity that I was on the way out, even before the selectors had met to pick the team. It had been common knowledge at a state second XI game a couple of weeks earlier. But to the end, I didn't believe they would do it.

"Have a good Christmas," I sneered to Jones and put the phone down.

Stillman rang that night, almost apologising for the decision. He was trying to justify it and I just listened. "It's unfortunate but Roachy's come in and that's the way it is."

I'd begun to understand what was happening. I started to realise that in standing up for myself and my teammates, I'd been pinned with the 'disloyal' tag. "You hung us out to dry at that meeting," I told Stillman. "You've filled Deano with shit. I don't know what your agenda is, but listen, you fucked with the wrong person when you fucked with me."

The words were threatening, but realistically, there wasn't much I could do.

I grabbed a stubby from the fridge and went for a walk around the streets of Richmond, where I was living at the time, and I was in tears. I thought my career was over. I was 25 and just 20-odd dismissals short of the state record, and I was finished. It hit me that the same thing had happened to Michael Dimattina all those years before. I walked up Bridge Road and turned past the swimming pool and I was thinking the darkest thoughts. My parents had gone, and my career had been taken from me and I wondered whether life was worth living. Right then and there I thought about taking my own life.

Fortunately Kath was at home at our flat when I got back. I lay on the bed upstairs and she said: "I can't understand how you're feeling. But I know cricket's everything to you. It'll turn around. It's unfair, what's happened and it will turn around." I had a dreadful Christmas, the first without my mother. Kath and I got in the car and just drove to get away from it, ending up at Apollo

Bay, on the surf coast. Kath advised me not to lash out and speak publicly, the best advice I ever had.

But others spoke out for me. Jones, Stillman and the chairman of selectors, John Grant, all said repeatedly that I'd been left out of the side because of poor batting. But a lot of people had trouble believing this, pointing to the fact I'd been averaging a respectable 32 that season. The affair became much bigger than whether Darren Berry should be in the team or not.

Shane Warne, who was away with the national team, had rung Jones and implored him not to do it. Warne also wrote a column in the *Sunday Age* in which he attacked Victoria, pointing to my good recent form. "How can that happen? He cannot have lost form in two weeks, so it must be something other than form. I am really disappointed that Berry has been dropped during his best season because of a personality clash."

Merv Hughes, who was also on the sidelines at the time and struggling to come to terms with the captain and coach, landed the biggest blow. In an interview with Malcolm Conn in *The Australian* newspaper, he said: "There may be a selection committee of five but it seems that over the years, anyone who had a disagreement with Les or isn't in Les's school of friends doesn't play too many games." Hughes was hauled in to the Victorian Cricket Association to explain his comments and given a suspended fine for speaking publicly about selection matters.

John Scholes told *The Age*: "Being the best wicketkeeper was the criteria for selection when I was there. Obviously that's changed." In the same newspaper, my co-author here, Martin Blake, commented: "Victorian cricket has a problem but contrary to what the selectors believe, it is not Darren Berry."

Michael Horan in the *Herald Sun* called my dumping "a hasty decision that suggests it is just not cricket that concerns the decision-makers". Linda Pearce, writing in the *Sunday Age*, also weighed in: "In Victorian cricket team-speak, Darren Berry is on the barbecue. He has fallen out of favour with the selectors who matter. He has been burned, sizzled, call it what you will."

Patrick Smith in *The Age* reported that Stillman would not be contracted when his term ran out at the end of the season. Brad Hodge, another who was on the outer, threatened to leave Victoria. "I think myself and Chuck are in the same position where we've got to wait and see what happens," he told the *Herald Sun*.

As you can see, this debate occupied weeks of time and reams of newsprint. During the match in Perth, I stood up on the hill at Apollo Bay to find some mobile phone reception so that I could call Horan in Perth to get some score updates, and just get a feel for the atmosphere from someone who was there. I had a cricketing form of separation anxiety. Roach made some more runs in that game, probably making Jones and Stillman breathe a little easier.

The whole thing was big news. Kath and myself were in the main street of the little beach town one day and as we walked past the pub a couple of guys hung their heads out the window and yelled : "Hey Roachy, how's it going, champ?" I laughed loudly, and Kath was pleased that at least I could laugh again.

I rang Jones in January after I heard him on radio, during a one-day match against Tasmania, saying that my omission was about batting and nothing more sinister. "You know it's political," I told him. "It's to do with us standing up to you. Roach was averaging 17 in club cricket when he was picked." I know that others tried to get to Jones behind the scenes. I know for a fact that my teammates Damien Fleming and Matthew Elliott pulled the skipper aside at state squad training one night, and told him that it was not me who organised the players' meeting; that Stillman had.

Deano wouldn't listen: "I know Chuck's behind this," he told them. Elliott came to my home before the next Shield game, against Tasmania, and told me he was not going to play because he was so upset about it. I told him that it was my problem and that he was being silly. He made a double-century.

My scrapbooks tell me that the newspapers regarded it as a stoush between me and Stillman, but it was the involvement of Jones which hurt the most. I wrote an epic letter to Deano in which I said that I had realised "how stupid and naïve I must have been to consider you a close friend of mine". I said my dropping from the team was "an assassination". For years afterward, we were estranged.

I will never forget my teammates Warne and Hughes putting their necks on the line for me that year. It showed me that friendship was more important than a game of cricket. Just about every member of the state squad rang me to commiserate. I drew on the support of my closest friends from the country Dennis Vague and his wife Gayle, Guy Freene (my best man) and his wife-to-be Jennie, my coach from back home Steve McNamara and his family, and of course Kath, who was my rock.

Ten years later I think that I understand the situation perfectly. Jones was going to be captain of Derbyshire in English county cricket over the winter, and Stillman had been hired to go in as coach alongside him. They couldn't afford to fall out. If the players were guilty of anything, it was complaining about Jones' treatment of us. It wasn't a mutiny, even if Jones and Stillman thought it was. I was devastated that Jones, someone I considered to be a friend, would not believe me when I looked him in the eye and told him that I was not after his job.

I also know that I took this too hard. At 34, I look back and I think: "What an idiot. There's more to life than a game of cricket." But the game was everything to me then. I guess I've learned a few of life's lessons and this was one of them.

* * *

I played out the season with Fitzroy-Doncaster, gradually regaining my resolve. A glance at the media would have told me that there was a chance of a change in the leadership, and Victoria finished on the bottom of the table in both competitions. By season's end, the newspapers were full of speculation that Jones was playing his last season for Victoria. He was already fielding an offer from a New Zealand province, one which he never took up. Jones attacked the VCA over the woeful practice facilities for the players, just as his predecessor, Simon O'Donnell, had done a few years earlier. Like O'Donnell, he found himself on the outer with authority. Martin Blake in *The Age* called for Jones to step down in the name of team harmony, for he had "lost the players", but to continue as a batsman because Victoria needed him.

Briefly, I considered moving to Zimbabwe to take up an offer and live my dream of playing Test cricket. Andy Flower, Zimbabwe's captain and a fine wicketkeeper-batsman, rang me in the New Year to ask if I was interested. I'd played league cricket against his brother Grant in 1992 and 1993 in England, and against Andy in a match for the Rest of The World at the Scarborough cricket festival. Flower told me he believed that because Zimbabwe had recently been admitted to the Test cricket family, the residential qualifying period would be just two years, as opposed to the usual four. He said that he wanted to focus on his batting, and give up the keeping.

I talked to Kath about it and it was an attractive suggestion. My career in Australia appeared to be over. I was young enough to wait the two years and still have a few good years of Test cricket. I'd asked Flower to check out the employment situation and what they could do for me. Kath and I had decided we would take the plunge. Then a couple of weeks later Flower rang back with bad news: "The qualifying period is four years," he said. "We still want you to come. But it's four years."

After some more thought, I turned him down. Realistically, I'd dreamed of playing Test cricket for Australia. Deep down, I felt an injustice had been done, and that I would win back my spot in the Victorian team. But I had no idea how, or more importantly when.

* * *

Dean Jones was relieved of Victoria's captaincy at the end of the 1995-96 season, and Les Stillman's contract as coach was not renewed. John Scholes was appointed as coach, and Shane Warne as captain for the first time. There would be a massive changing of the guard.

Jones lost several friendships over the events of that awful season, including Merv Hughes'. I can remember Deano charging down the track and smashing Merv's bowling in a trial game that year, and calling him a "fat @#$@#" and a medium-pacer, and telling him he couldn't bowl, and I can remember cringing because there were young, up-and-coming players listening to this exchange between two household names and Test cricketers. Merv did have the last laugh that day, dismissing his old mate and quietly sending him on his way.

One of Victoria's greatest players, Dean Jones is a mass of contradictions. He could be gruff like he was that day against Merv Hughes, but for years as his roommate and friend I defended him when colleagues and friends accused him of arrogance. Deano had a fearful reputation for turning conversations around to himself, and behind his back, people mockingly referred to him as 'Legend'. I would tell them that there was another side to him that I had seen, a side that the public did not see. He was so good to me when my mother died and Kath and I would occasionally go out to Romsey where he lived to have dinner with him and his wife Jane. I knew that beneath the off-hand and arrogant exterior, he was a sensitive, caring person.

Stillman coached me for seven years and all the while he had problems with communication. He'd come to me and say: "Lehmann's too fat. He won't get a game until he gets fit." But then he'd go to Lehmann later and say: "Chuck's got to get some runs or he won't get a game." He didn't seem to understand that most of us were mates, and that his criticism would get back to the player. Or maybe he did understand and it was his way of getting the message across.

Ultimately the trust in the team broke down and the level of animosity toward him bubbled until Wayne Phillips, captaining the team one day at the MCG, pulled us together in a huddle as we walked on to the ground. Phillips was a mild-mannered character, but he'd had enough: "Don't worry about him in the dressing room. Let's play this game for this group of players right here."

Stillman served two more years than he should have had, because the VCA had no idea of the level of disenchantment about his coaching. We speak when we cross paths nowadays, but not much more than that. I didn't like Stillman's style. I preferred the way David Hookes operated, which was to tell you bluntly and straight to your face what he wanted. Hookes told me that he wanted Cameron White to captain Victoria's one-day team in

2003-04 and he openly questioned my future in the team. It worried me, but at least I knew where I stood.

Stillman and Jones went to Derbyshire and endured a player uprising led by Dominic Cork, the English Test player, the following year. I must admit, I felt a little vindication at this point. It doesn't make me right or wrong. It just means that we weren't the only ones who had problems with their methods.

One final point is worth mentioning. When I retired, I got a nice message from Dean Jones, which goes to show that time definitely does heal a few wounds. "You've had a great career, Chuck," he said. I was touched. Not so long ago, he called me up and at his suggestion; we went down to Richmond and had a coffee. The events of the past 12 months have made me realise that life is too short to hold grudges.

CHAPTER 9 COMEBACK

My 10-month exile from the Victorian cricket team was a time of close self-examination. Towards the end of that 1995-96 season I'd become mentally strong again, despite my absence from the team. It was a time that taught me some hard lessons and a period where I reassessed where I wanted to go in life. I began a university degree to become a physical education teacher, realising that I needed some security outside the game of cricket. My time out of the side, whilst difficult, also gave me some perspective on life.

During the off season I'd made a hard decision and left my original district club Fitzroy-Doncaster to join Northcote, The decision was one of the hardest decisions I ever made in my career. Fitzroy-Doncaster had given me a wonderful opportunity by starting me as a 17-year-old in the first XI without having to climb through the grades as most youngsters do. When my career had stalled at state level, I was looking for a new challenge. This came in the form of an offer to be assistant coach and vice-captain with Northcote. After meeting with coach Mick O' Sullivan and President Ross McKenzie, I was convinced a change of clubs was just what I needed as a fresh start.

Gary and Leigh Watts, who had played their entire careers at Fitzroy, were less than impressed I had decided to switch clubs and let me know about it in no uncertain terms. This upset me a lot, because both these men had played a big part in my development as a player. Part of me felt as though I had let down my friend and mentor George Murray, who had recruited me. I drove out to his house to tell him face to face of my decision and I could tell he was disappointed.

The move to Northcote was based on a fresh start and also on the back of the respect I had for a few of the players at the club. Grant Gardiner and Gerard Dowling were two men I really admired for their attitude to the game. Both of them were role models for me, just as the Watts brothers had been at Fitzroy-Doncaster. Dowling and Gardiner were the ultimate professionals, squeezing every ounce out of the ability they were given. I was proud to play alongside both men for Victoria as well as in a club premiership in that first season with Northcote. The grand final, played at the Albert Ground, provided me with a personal highlight when I scored 109 in our total of 404. Tim O' Sullivan and I put on a record 115 for the 6th wicket to set up the victory.

My subsequent years at Northcote were enjoyable although not as fruitful as the first year. Long time club president Dr Chand Jain—simply known as 'Doc'—returned to his beloved club at the start of that premiership year and we formed a friendship I value enormously.

Doc is of Indian descent and like most Indians is fanatical about the game. He has put his heart and soul into Northcote Cricket Club over many years until recently, due to ill health, he stepped aside. The club seems to be missing something since he left. His passion and enthusiasm was unbridled, along with his humour which has given me plenty to laugh about during my career.

One other thing I did to help myself was to call Kevin Sheedy, the great Essendon mentor whose long stint as an AFL coach was legendary. Sheedy also was a handy cricketer in his day, and I'd always respected him, so I thought it worthwhile to seek him out for a chat.

Kevin had heard of my situation and he agreed to see me the day after I called him. We met at the Old Melbourne Hotel for lunch, and I was quite nervous. It was a strange meeting in a sense, because for the next two hours he kept writing down notes about everything I said.

I walked away a little bemused. I'd gone to seek some advice from the great Kevin Sheedy, yet he seemed to have asked more questions of me! But I did take at least one positive message from that meeting. "Do you believe in yourself?" he had asked me. "Because if you do, it doesn't matter who's in your way, you'll get back in the team. As soon as you start doubting yourself, your career is finished."

I did believe in myself and events in the boardroom were working in my favour. The Victorian Cricket Association had removed Jones as captain and Stillman as coach over the off-season. Even more importantly, they had appointed John 'Barrel' Scholes, my old club coach and mentor, as state coach, and given my good friend Shane Warne his first taste of the captaincy for the 1996-97 season.

It seemed fairly obvious that I had a good chance of redeeming myself now, although Scholes would not give any guarantees. He had been a great source of strength for me during my time on the sidelines, speaking out publicly against the elevation of Peter Roach above me, and privately counselling me. Barrel had told me during the dark times of his own period out of the state team after he'd captained Victoria at 21, only to find himself out of favour for a few seasons, and then returning to complete a fine career. "Don't chuck it in now," he'd told me. "Don't crack up and lose your chance. Work on your game and make sure you're a better player when you come back."

While the Victorian players endured their pre-season campaign for the 1996-97 season, Scholes told me that I would be head-to-head with Roach. "You know that I think you're the best wicketkeeper. But I'll be one of four people (selectors) making the decision."

The good vibes I was getting proved correct. When Victoria sent a team to a Super 8s tournament in north Queensland in the pre-season, I was selected as wicketkeeper. In the first one-day match of the season, against Tasmania, I was picked ahead of Roach for a game which Jones and Warne dominated.

In November the Sheffield Shield season began in Sydney and I was back in the Victorian team again and chuffed about it. I'd thought my career over. Now I was determined not to give anyone a chance to displace me again. I'd worked on my batting while I was away from the team, having private coaching and toiling away in the nets. In that game against New South Wales, it would come to fruition.

It was an important game for me. There was still some controversy around about my dumping and then my reinstatement to the team, so a few runs were not going to hurt. I missed out in the first innings, and then in the second dig, we were set a massive 456 to win, a task made all the more difficult when we slumped to 5/89.

On the evening of the third day of the game, the Victorian players went to a pub to watch Evander Holyfield fight Mike Tyson for the world heavyweight championship of boxing. Tyson was considered unbeatable at the time, but Holyfield won in a major boilover. Leaving the pub that night, I looked at Matthew

Elliott: "Hey, no one thought Holyfield would beat Tyson. We need 350 to win. Who knows? Miracles happen. We've just watched one."

The following day was one of the most amazing of my career. We began the final day at 5/100 and survived until lunch, then flourished in the afternoon against a Blues' attack that boasted three spinners – Stuart MacGill, David Freedman and Greg Matthews. Elliott passed 100, and in the afternoon I whipped Steve Waugh through mid-wicket to reach my maiden first class century. Waugh had been at me throughout: "You're not up to it. It'd be an injustice for you to get 100, Chuck." To his credit, he was generous in his praise when I waved my bat to the dressing room and the sparse crowd. Dropped from the side – apparently for poor batting – I'd returned with a century in my first game back.

But the game was there to be won. We ploughed on into the final session and took the score to 5/379, needing just 77 to win and with some more batting (Paul Reiffel, Shane Warne, Brad Williams and Damien Fleming) to come. We overtook the Victorian sixth-wicket record of 289, set 50 years earlier by Sam Loxton and Doug Ring. Elliott surged on to 187 but was bowled by a ball from MacGill that turned viciously, and he left the field with his head in his hands. Now I knew that I would have to be the man to carry Victoria home. But a few minutes later I pushed half-forward at Freedman and was out lbw for 148 from 250 balls, with 17 fours.

Writing in *The Age*, Peter Roebuck called us "Burke and Wills", and his imagery was appropriate. Victoria got to touching distance, but fell over and lost. Elliott and I were shattered to think we were so close but so far. "The result's everything," I told the press afterward.

But there is no doubt that game was a turning point for me as well as being one of the best matches I ever played in. It turned out to be my best-ever season statistically, with 590 runs at 31.00 and 45 dismissals. In the second match of the season, against South Australia at the MCG, I took seven catches and made a stumping as SA was skittled for 84. My eight dismissals equalled the Australian record for a single innings and with three catches in the second innings, my total of 11 dismissals equalled the Victorian record I had set against Pakistan the season before.

Again at the MCG, I hit the winning runs to defeat Tasmania in a cliffhanger, belting Colin Miller through the covers for four and in the process reaching my half-century. Damien Fleming and I extracted the last 20 runs so that we won by a single wicket. I distinctly remember David Boon, the Tasmanian captain, being filthy that we had got up and won a nailbiter.

In December our acting captain Tony Dodemaide broke a finger and could not play against Queensland, leaving the selectors with a difficult decision about the captaincy. To my chagrin, they went back to Jones for that game. Not only was it a bad decision, but it was unfair on Jones, who'd been removed only a few months earlier.

During that game at the Gabba I finally overtook Richie Robinson's Victorian wicketkeeping record of 265 dismissals, a landmark I'd been approaching early in the previous season before I was dumped. I had five catches and a stumping in the Queensland first innings, including one of the best snares of my career, high, right and in one glove to catch Martin Love from Brad Williams' bowling. When I landed I was on the right hand side of Laurie Harper, who was at first slip.

We finished fifth in the Shield competition and fourth in the one-dayers. But I thought we were better than that.

* * *

At the end of that season, Tony Dodemaide, one of my favourite Victorian players, retired, leaving open a leadership position within the team. Victoria appointed me as vice-captain to Shane Warne for the 1997-98 season, a huge honour. I knew that Warney would be away a fair bit of the time; it was captaincy without the title.

I'd been away to England in the winter and been called up to the Australian team for the last seven weeks of the Ashes tour, the highlight of my career. My stocks were up when the season began.

But it was a bad season for various reasons. The fallout from my problems with Dean Jones from two seasons before came back to haunt me. It was a rocky road.

Initially, Deano was fine. But then we started to play games and I began making decisions as captain, he could not cope with it. I'm sure he was uncomfortable with his young, former roommate now telling him what to do. He was still blaming me for his sacking and it was an eye-for-an-eye situation.

My first game as captain was against New Zealand at Optus Oval, and we won easily behind a 10-wicket haul from David Saker. I was rapt for Saker, a good friend and premiership teammate at club level with Northcote. He was the form bowler in the country at the time, and was very unlucky not to play in the Boxing Day Test soon afterwards. The selectors instead chose Western Australian Matthew Nicholson to replace the injured Glenn McGrath and Sakers chance passed him by.

Deano was sulking during the New Zealand game, off to the side of the group during the warm-ups, and I wasn't happy with him. Neither was Scholes. I asked Deano to practise some catches because I wanted him to field in the slips cordon, and he just ignored me and walked off the ground.

"Listen, for this to work it's not about Dean Jones, it's not about Darren Berry, it's about the Victorian team. Let's get on with it," I told him. "Worry about your game and I'll worry about mine," came the response.

It was uncomfortable to say the least. Give Deano credit, he was one of the best fieldsman I played with or against. But in that game, he chased balls out to the boundary at three-quarter pace. He made it a very public statement and the players were well aware of it. But I tried my best to ignore it because I didn't want it to affect the team.

I had another dispute with him when we played a one-dayer at the Gabba against Queensland. Deano had told us he wanted to open the batting. In the nets, he was running down the track and slogging every bowler while the team management talked about his proposal. It was ridiculous. I went into the nets and I'm thinking: "How can I tell Dean Jones how to play?" I walked in there and I said: "Listen, you're not opening the batting. Can you start batting sensibly? You're our best player. We want you to bat where you always bat, at No. 3, and play the usual Dean Jones role." He said: "Don't tell me how to play."

It all came to a head during the Shield game in Perth at the start of March. I knew that Deano wasn't going to give me an easy ride because he'd been sacked. Once again in Perth he was irritated. We did this circle drill in the warm-up, where the keeper throws the ball out to a fieldsman and calls out "keeper" or "bowler" and he has to throw it to either end. Jones was hurling it at my end as hard as he could from 20 metres away. I would have broken a hand if I'd taken his throws, so I just let them go. I'd given the whole thing a chance to settle, but I'd had enough now. A few players were becoming upset with his behaviour.

I followed him into the rooms: "Deano, I want to see you out the back right now."

We went out the back of the rooms at the WACA Ground and had a heated discussion which at one point, almost came to blows. I told Deano that if he continued to act in that manner, there was no point him taking the field with us. His angry response was along the lines of: "Good, I don't want to be out there anyway."

I told him we would take Shaun Craig, our 12th man, out on to the field. Craig came out to field and the management made up a story about Jones having a stomach upset, so that his absence was explained. The truth is that we didn't want him out there and he didn't want to be there either. Scholes went to speak to him, and after a while he ran out on to the field and his attitude had changed.

We finished second-last in the Shield and seventh in the one-dayers. It was a dreadful season and once again, it was a Victorian team that did not gel. The final straw for me came late in the season when Jones walked out of the dressing room at the MCG and in front of everyone, took off his Victorian cap and jumper and threw them in a bin. Brad Hodge, who'd idolised Deano, went to fetch them out.

"Don't you dare!" I told him.

* * *

Dean Jones, one of the greatest players Victoria ever had, retired before the 1998-99 season. Deano had been overlooked by the national selectors for a few years, and his problems in Victoria are well-documented here. We had finished second-last or last in each of the three previous years and it is no secret that our inability to find any real team spirit had contributed to the poor results.

Scholes had worked hard as coach to restore some camaraderie and faith in Victoria over the previous two years but it was quite obvious that so long as Jones and I were there together it was going to be difficult. Suddenly Scholes' job became a little easier. But all along, he had said it might take a couple of years to restore the values he wanted within the team.

We had our best season for some time in 1998-99, finishing third in the Shield, and just missing out on the final. We unearthed a good player in the left-arm swing bowler Mathew Inness, who marked his debut for Victoria by holding on at No. 11 to make 27 in a last-wicket stand of 118 with me against New South Wales at the MCG, helping me to an unbeaten 166, my highest first class score. It was evident to me that we'd found a beauty, a bloke with the character you needed to play at this level. He has a heart as big as Phar Lap.

We were virtually in the final at lunch on the last day of our final game against Western Australia, but we couldn't shift Rob Baker and Simon Katich and WA ended up hanging on. Otherwise we might have won the double. We took out the Mercantile Mutual Cup one-day final against a New South Wales team captained by Mark Taylor. We didn't have a star-studded team but we did have effective players like Laurie Harper, David Saker and Jason Bakker, who had a prime role in both our one-day titles during this period.

I was enjoying the captaincy perhaps for the first time. I believed it was a myth that wicketkeepers could not captain the side. As a keeper, you knew when the bowlers were struggling. It was the best seat in the house as far as I was concerned.

Better still, things were turning around for Victoria.

CHAPTER 10 THE ASHES '97

If 1995 was the bottom of the barrel for me, then 1997 was the best of years. In April, Kath and I were married in Melbourne surrounded by family and friends. It was an emotional time, because my parents were not around to witness the occasion. My mother's two wishes for me had been that I be happily married, and that I play cricket for Australia. As it happened, both would come to fruition in the same year.

Our honeymoon would be in England, where we stayed with Andrew Towle, my old captain at Macclesfield, who had been in the wedding party. The Cheshire league had banned overseas professionals a couple of years earlier, so I was coaching the club rather than playing, and all the while enjoying my honeymoon. It was a fairly informal arrangement. Using Cheshire as a base, we travelled to Spain, Italy and other European countries between cricket matches. It's like going to Adelaide or Hobart for a weekend.

Australia was touring England for an Ashes series in that year with Ian Healy and Adam Gilchrist as the two keepers, and beneath the surface, part of me knew that if there was an injury, then the fact I was in the country might help my cause for a

AUSTRALIAN CRICKET BOARD

16 July 1997

Mr Darren BERRY

YALLAMBIE VIC 3085

Dear Darren

1997 COCA-COLA ASHES TOUR

I am pleased to detail the arrangements for the current Ashes Tour.

Kindly read the information provided below and note any items which require follow up and give them your immediate attention.

1. **TOUR PARTY**

Mark TAYLOR	(NSW)	Captain
Steve WAUGH	(NSW)	Vice-Captain
Darren BERRY	(VIC)	
Michael BEVAN	(NSW)	
Greg BLEWETT	(SA)	
Matthew ELLIOTT	(Vic)	
Jason GILLESPIE	(SA)	
Ian HEALY	(Qld)	
Brendon JULIAN	(WA)	
Michael KASPROWICZ	(Qld)	
Justin LANGER	(WA)	
Glenn McGRATH	(NSW)	
Ricky PONTING	(Tas)	
Paul REIFFEL	(Vic)	
Michael SLATER	(NSW)	
Shane WARNE	(Vic)	
Mark WAUGH	(NSW)	
Manager:	Alan CROMPTON (NSW)	
Coach:	Geoff MARSH (WA)	
Physiotherapist:	Errol ALCOTT (NSW)	
Fitness Adviser:	Steve SMITH (WA)	
Scorer:	Mike WALSH (Vic)	

Tour Selection Committee: Captain, Vice-Captain, Coach

call-up. Wade Seccombe, the Queensland keeper, was in England as well, probably with the same thought process. It's about the off-chance. Certainly I'd tossed the keeping gloves in the suitcase just in case.

The opportunity came during the third Test at Old Trafford, Manchester. I lived 20 minutes from the famous, old ground and I'd gone to see the cricket on the first day. The Old Trafford Test is a social gathering for virtually every one of the dozens of Australian cricketers who ply their trade in England over our winter, and this was no exception. As is his style, the former Victorian all-rounder Brendan McArdle had managed to squeeze perhaps 50 people into the members' bar in the pavilion using a grand total of about four tickets. McArdle had spent almost every winter for 20 years playing in England and placing young cricketers at clubs there, and he was a good friend, as well as the greatest ticket-scammer in the Western world.

I was there having a few beers with a couple of mates from Macclesfield when McArdle and a former Victorian teammate, Geoff Allardice, proceeded to tell me that Gilchrist, Healy's backup, had injured a knee during the warm-up and that it looked serious. Not only that, the Australian selector Steve Bernard was looking for me. Initially, I thought they were cranking me up. But Mark Ray, a journalist friend of mine, confirmed the news, and my heart-rate would have tripled at that moment. I ran into Bernard late in the day, and I knew something was on. "I've got to catch up with you tomorrow," he said.

By the end of the second day of the Test match, the team management had apparently completed their analysis of Gilchrist's injury, and Bernard found me in the bar, telling me that if Gilly needed to return to Australia, then I would be called up. He told me to keep it quiet for now, until they decided whether it would be on a standby basis, under which I'd be called into specific games and then return to Cheshire, or whether I would replace Gilchrist as a full-time member of the squad and travel with the team.

Shane Warne had taken five wickets that day and equalled Richie Benaud's record as the leading leg-spinner in Australian cricket, so my mates and I adjourned to the Copthorne Hotel, where the team was staying, to catch up with Warney. I couldn't contain myself and I told him my news. He said that there was a whisper in the dressing room, but advised me not to get my hopes up. It was good advice, because I'd missed out a few times before.

But at 11am on the next morning, a Saturday, I was preparing to coach Macclesfield when Alan Crompton, the Australian team manager, called me at Towle's home. Crompton said I was officially being called up to the team and that I needed to be at Old Trafford the next day to go through some logistics. I was beside myself. Crompton seemed to be concerned about my ability to extract myself from Macclesfield. He had no idea how informal the arrangement was. "I'm coach and they'll release me today," I told him, rather panicked.

That day I went to the cricket at Warrington and used Towle's mobile phone to ring everyone who mattered at home. Sadly, Kath had gone home to Melbourne for work a few days earlier. But I called her and John Scholes and my family. That night we all went to the usual curry house in Macclesfield and the champagne flowed. The lads from Macclesfield couldn't believe their coach was about to join the all-conquering Aussie team. I reckon they were as happy as I was.

I met coach Geoff Marsh and Crompton on the Sunday, and they talked through financial matters and told me I would be part of the touring team for the rest of the trip. I was to receive a set fee for the last eight weeks of the tour, plus a share of the prizemoney. I said: "I couldn't give a shit how much you're paying me. I've just come to play for Australia." There were three Tests remaining against England, plus trips to Scotland and Northern Ireland.

The management seemed to be convinced that I'd been *playing* cricket in England, when the reality was that I'd only played a handful of hit-and-giggle games in borrowed gear. But I wasn't about to tell them otherwise. Then there was the awful moment when they told me to get my gear. I'd called up my sponsor, Gray Nicolls, and asked for some new equipment to be sent. But on my first day as an Australian player, I had nothing but my trusty wicketkeeping gloves. I had no pants, no pads, no spikes. I rang John Scholes in Melbourne and asked him to go around to our home in Yallambie and break into the house to get my stuff. But Scholes rang back later to say that he hadn't been able to get into the house. I would have to borrow the gear on the quiet until Gray Nicolls came through.

That night Alan Crompton took me upstairs to this quiet room at Old Trafford and presented me with the baggy, green cap of Australia, just a cricket cap in reality, but symbolically one of the most powerful images in the world of cricket. I don't think Crompton appreciated how much it meant to me. I was like a kid on Christmas day with his first bicycle. There was a tear in my eye and I was thinking of Mum and Dad and how they would have loved to have been there.

Crompton left me to my thoughts, and later I went downstairs to barrack Australia to victory in the Test match. It was a famous victory inspired by Steve Waugh's pair of centuries on a difficult pitch, and the scenes in the dressing rooms will be with me forever. Of course I'd heard of Ian Healy leading the players in the team song, Underneath the Southern Cross, but to be part of it was something else. I felt awkward, because I'd only just been added to the squad. Gilchrist was there, and clearly upset to be going home, which added to my discomfort. Gilly hadn't played

Test cricket to this point, and was in the queue, just like me. To his credit, Warne draped an arm around me and drew me into the circle. "Come on. You're in the Australian team now!" he said.

Mark Taylor, the captain, put an arm around me on the other side. "Can you believe it?" he said. "Surrounded by Victorians!" The hairs on the back of my neck stood to attention as we belted it out:

> *"Underneath the Southern Cross I stand*
> *A sprig of wattle in my hand*
> *A native of my native land*
> *Australia ... You Fucking Beauty!"*

Much to the boys' displeasure, we took the bus straight to Newcastle that night for a game starting the next morning against the Minor Counties at Jesmond, a relatively low-key affair. My first official team meal was drive-through McDonalds, an irony considering the image of the national team as enjoying the high life! On the bus, they tried to string a team together, with considerable difficulty. No one seemed too interested, with the exception of the little bloke from Wonthaggi. "I'll play," I said. Brendon Julian, my room mate in Newcastle, must have questioned my sanity as I stood in front of the mirror that night, admiring the mythical symbol on my head, tilting it this way and that for effect.

Of all the grounds to begin my career under the baggy green it had to be Jesmond. Four years earlier, I'd played for a Rest of the World invitational XI against England at the very same ground, and Mum, who'd flown over to England, came to see it. I could remember where she sat that day, and as I walked out on to that ground pulling that cap down on my head and fidgeting with my gloves, I could see her there again. I kissed my wedding ring and my Mum's wedding ring, which I was wearing on a necklace, and went out to play for my country. It was a special day for me in more ways than one.

Considering the lack of preparation, I was happy with my performance. I wicketkept for Australia for the first time in a pair of pads borrowed from the keeper at Macclesfield, and wearing a teammate's shoes. Ian Healy had loaned me a pair of half-spikes in the morning, up in his hotel room, a little bleary-eyed. "Enjoy yourself," he'd said, and handed me the shoes. But when I got to the ground, there was a problem. He'd given me two right shoes. As previously mentioned, I am anal about my gear and at this point, I panicked. Healy, who admitted later in the tour that he'd set me up, must have been rolling around his bed with laughter back at the hotel. I found some shoes that fitted, got 34 with the bat, and took my first catch, appropriately from Paul Reiffel's bowling, and loved every instant of it.

My new gear had arrived by the time we played John Paul Getty's XI at the billionaire philanthropist's private ground in Buckinghamshire, in the south of England, and it was an amazing day. Getty's cricket ground was without doubt the best and most beautiful I've ever seen anywhere. He had something like 10 groundsmen and everything was pristine. It was spot-the-celebrity in the crowd. Mick Jagger was there, as well as John Major, the former British Prime Minister. The opposition had Robin Smith, Martin Crowe, Derek Randall and Alex Tudor, a promising English quick bowler who put a few under Mark Taylor's nose. I batted a while with the skipper, got 20-odd not out and was left with another indelible memory.

At Cardiff, in Wales, I made my first class debut for Australia. I copped an awful caught-behind decision in the second innings when I'd set myself to get some runs, and I was filthy. But I had a good game with the gloves, highlighted by a difficult leg-side stumping from Michael Bevan's bowling and a few catches from Michael Kasprowicz.

The tour went back to London where we were to play Middlesex at Lord's. Of course I was desperate to play at the home of cricket, but Heals said he needed the practice, so I had to step aside. A highlight of that few days was our visit to meet the Queen at Buckingham Palace, and what struck me was that guys like Taylor and Steve Waugh, who'd played top-level cricket in front of big crowds, were nervous. We had morning tea and lined up to meet the Queen. Heals gave her a painting that his infant daughter had done, saying that she had asked for it to be handed to Her Majesty. "Do you reckon she's got it up on the fridge?" we chided him that night.

The Test series was level at 1-1 with three matches remaining, and we tripped up to Leeds for the fourth Test at the Headingley ground. Me, Kasper and Justin Langer worked on our fitness while the others played, and I looked upon this time as good pre-season training for me. I'd lost about five kilograms of puppy fat stacked on over my honeymoon. Matthew Elliott had made a brilliant 199 in our victory, and once again, my abiding memory is from the celebrations. The Australian team had an environment and a feel that was almost completely foreign to me. It was a sensational environment in which to play cricket, so much different from the chemistry I'd experienced in most of my Victorian teams to that point. I was aware there had been some rumblings about Mark Taylor's spot in the side because of his run of poor form until he'd made an early century in the Test series, and I heard the talk among the players. But it wasn't malicious. This was a team that got along.

After we cleaned up the Poms, a few guys from the Canberra Raiders rugby league team – big Mal Meninga, Laurie Daley and Ricky Stuart — came into the little dressing rooms and the place went off. About 10 o'clock we were still there and we sat around in a circle and Steve Waugh put John Williamson's *True Blue* on the ghetto blaster so that we could all sing it. This team knew how to win and they knew how to celebrate a win.

At Trent Bridge, Nottingham, we won the fifth Test to secure the Ashes. I filled my time commentating on the BBC at their invitation, joining Jonathon Agnew, Henry Blofeld and Neville Oliver on the air to talk about keeping to Warne and the methods used by Healy. I also ran into one of my childhood heroes, Bob Taylor, at the Test match, and we went into the nets to do a session together, which was interesting and informative. Once again, the celebrations were huge. It was the best vibe I'd known in any team.

After a game against Ireland near Derry, where I collected five catches and a stumping from the previously-unknown bowling talent of one Mark Taylor, I played another first class match against Kent at Canterbury. Those few days were interesting for the fact that the players held meetings with Tim May, president of the new Australian Cricketers' Association, which was about to enter negotiations with the Australian Cricket Board for a collective bargaining agreement. It was a time of a certain amount of unrest, especially in relation to the wages paid to Sheffield Shield players who were required to commit full-time over summer so that normal employment became impossible. Within a year, it would be front page news around the country and the game would come close to its first full-on strike by players.

But for now there were a few grumblings. We learned that James Erskine, the entrepreneur, would handle the negotiations with the ACB. My own situation caused some discussion, because it was felt I wasn't being paid the appropriate fee. Steve

Waugh was very strong on this, and Warney was upset, but from my point of view, I would have been there for nothing.

For nearly eight weeks, the best eight weeks of my life, I'd kept well when I had the opportunity. I'd done everything I could to break Ian Healy's hand, from smashing catches at him in the warm-ups, to feigning to trip him as he alighted from a double-decker bus. In truth, you'd never wish an injury on anyone, let alone a teammate. But it was good fun. "Come on Heals," I'd say with a big grin. "Break a hand. Give us a crack!"

"Don't be like that, Chucky," he'd say.

Once the warrior Healy walked out with the Australian team to play the sixth and final Test match at The Oval in London, I knew that my tour was over from a playing point of view. I did some commentary with the BBC again, a portent of things to come. But Phil Tufnell and Andrew Caddick knocked us over in a small second-innings run chase and we lost, leaving the series at 3-2 our way. It was a flattering result for England.

A couple of things stick in my mind. There was a relaxed air in the dressing room and on the last day, Taylor, Warne, Shane Lee and Shaun 'China' Young had the cards out playing 500 and were having a laugh. Steve Waugh was waiting to bat, and he went ballistic. "We've got the Test match won have we? There's a Test match going on out there!" There was no such thing as a "dead rubber" for Stephen Waugh.

Young was playing his first and only Test match after Paul Reiffel had returned to Australia for family reasons, and with Jason Gillespie breaking down. I was pleased for China, whom I'd come to know as a fine player in first class ranks. But I had to laugh at the boys winding him up, telling him that he had to wear the cap everywhere on the first day, out of respect for tradition.

Young took them on their word; wore it on the bus and wouldn't take it off. He had no clue.

The other thing that comes back to me is Ian Botham's arrival in our rooms for a chat while we chased those runs. Ray Phillips, our liaison officer, was filling the bathtub with ice and champagne and beer, and Botham smiled. "The game's over is it boys? The last time you blokes did this, I belted the shit out of you at Headingley!" Of course he was referring to one of cricket's most famous matches, the Test at Leeds in 1981 when England followed on but then beat Australia behind Botham's whirlwind 149 and Bob Willis' eight wickets.

Botham smiled and winked at me as I passed him on the way up to the balcony at The Oval for the presentations. England had won. "Funny game, cricket," I said.

This tour was the culmination of everything in cricket for me. I was so close to Test cricket that I could touch it. Geoff Marsh gave me a good report and I thought: "I'm close." Alas, seven more years wouldn't take me any closer.

The trip ended in farce and hilarity. Mark Waugh and Elliott had spent a lot of time baiting each other about how slow the other was between the wickets. It was this pair, remember, who'd crashed into each other – wrecking Elliott's knee and stalling his career – in a Test at Sydney nine months earlier. "I'd beat you every time over 100 metres," Elliott would say to the New South Welshman.

Around 10 o'clock, we were still in the rooms, and I drunkenly suggested a run-off on the ground between Elliott and Waugh. I added that it should be done in the nude. Elliott had the kit off straight away, but not Waugh, who had a modest side to his character. In the end, a few of us went down to the ground and the run-off became a naked lap of one of the oldest cricket grounds in the world, scene of so many famous days of cricket. I joined half a dozen players in the jaunt. Justin Langer placed a strategic sponsor's sticker that protected his privacy but proved difficult to remove later. I've never laughed so much.

We'd just lost the Test match to the old enemy, by the way. But we were going home.

CHAPTER 11 A MAN CALLED SHANE WARNE

The question I am asked most in my life in cricket circles is: "What's Shane Warne really like?" It's not necessarily a simple question to answer, but I'll try.

Firstly from a cricket perspective, I have been lucky enough to wicketkeep to the greatest leg-spin bowler ever and along with Ian Healy and Adam Gilchrist, I consider that a great honour. It is something that I will probably appreciate even more as the years go by. When I look back on my career I will be proud to say I played in the same era as Shane Keith Warne.

It was always a challenge keeping to him as you never knew exactly when one would rip past the outside edge and present you with a chance. His strong, thick fingers, I believe, are his secret weapon and have helped make him the champion that he is. His big spinning leggies and drift are the two things that have caused batsmen around the world the most headaches.

He also possesses a lethal flipper, which is a ball not many bowlers can perfect. If he has a weakness, I would say it is his wrong-'un. I found it easy to pick, and it has never really spun that much. In saying that, he bamboozled a lot of left-handers with it as well as his slider, which floated out like a leggie but went straight on and left many a mollydooker confused. He has changed the game with his sheer brilliance and I was lucky enough to have the best seat in the house when he pulled on the Big V cap.

Warney and I have been friends for 15 years, and during that time we have both faced some very difficult times, as well as sharing some truly wonderful moments. It's not that often that you share a friendship with a person who goes on to be very successful in his chosen field — let me rephrase that – becomes the best ever.

Our friendship began in the late 80s at various under-age training squads, but really blossomed during the Australian under 21 tour of the West Indies in 1990. We have a lot in common, but also are opposites in many ways. His smoking has always been my pet hate, and he knows it. He regularly would drop ash in my corner of the dressing room just to piss me off, given my obsession with tidiness. I am very neat and tidy and Shane is terribly messy, and for these two reasons we always had some good arguments as roommates on tour.

We both have a passion for the St Kilda Football Club, which is funny, because as a young boy I followed Fitzroy, and Warney followed Hawthorn. We rarely admit to that. We both played in the under 19s for St Kilda as teenagers, and our passion for the club grew from there. Whenever we can, we get along to the games and support the club in full voice. I spent some time — albeit brief — as the runner at the start of the 2003 season and Warney has been involved in various leadership group meetings and developed a friendship with a few of the players. I look forward to the day the Saints climb their Everest and lift the premiership cup aloft, and you can bet that the two of us will be there with our autograph books acting like little kids.

One of my first memories of the bottle blonde from Black Rock (although he is originally from Ferntree Gully) is of him pulling into the Junction Oval in St Kilda in his white Cortina with the music blaring. It was like a mobile disco. He has always had a love of music, the louder the better, and his taste is usually of the top-40 chart stuff. He still loves loud music and I honestly believe deep down he would love to have been a rock star.

Warney's other passion is cars. He has had more cars in his time than he has had hot dinners. From humble beginnings in the Cortina, he has graduated through the motor industry to his pride and joy, his silver Ferrari. At one ugly stage a few years back he actually purchased a Brock Commodore with all the trimmings. This caused quite a stir in the Warne household, as Shane's wife Simone was less than impressed. She referred to it as the "Bogan-mobile" and refused to travel in the noisy thing. Once again Shane's true colours were shining through; he's certainly got an element of 'bogan' in his make-up.

He is an enormously proud person and loves to show you his new toys, just like a little kid on Christmas day. It doesn't matter if it's a new car, laptop computer, clothing, music system or house, he delights in showing off his new purchases to anyone who will give him the time to look and listen. He makes me laugh at times with how the simple things in life give him great pleasure and he is certainly a no frills man when it comes to what he eats. Yet at other times, he lives life like a Hollywood superstar. The honest truth about Warney is that he is at heart a basic Aussie bloke who loves a smoke and a pizza, but who happens to have become the greatest leg-spin bowler the world has ever seen and therefore a megastar in this country.

I remember in one of his early Shield games we returned from an interstate trip and met up with the wives and girlfriends at the Redback brewery pub in North Melbourne. Upon arrival I introduced him to my girlfriend (now wife) Katherine and for some stupid reason, he called her 'Christine'. Kath, having no idea who he was, responded with: "Hello Shaun." It was a hilarious moment and one that has remained with them for years. They still refer to each other as Shaun and Christine.

Our two families have developed a strong relationship over the years, with our wives being good friends, and now that we both have children this will undoubtedly develop further. Shane's parents Keith and Brigitte are two of the nicest people you could ever meet. They have supported Shane through his good and bad times, and I know how much Warney appreciates his parents. They are very close, along with his brother Jason, who now helps Warney with his commercial dealings.

During the drugs ban in 2003 I really felt for Keith and Brigitte, especially his Mum, who was unfortunately dragged into the whole situation. Sure, Warney did get the diuretics from his mother, but it wasn't her fault what was to follow. Shane was the one at fault for taking the tablets and at no stage did he blame his Mum, but some sections of the media portrayed it in that manner.

As cricketers, we are well aware that before we take or are prescribed any medication we need to check exactly the contents of the product. He was a little naïve to ignore this rule when he decided to pop a few of him Mum's diuretics. Everyone asks me: "Why did he do it? Is he a drug cheat? Was it for his shoulder injury?"

I would like to go on record as saying that Shane Warne is not a drug cheat and he didn't take those pills as a masking agent for anything else. Warney took the pills purely and simply to lose some weight, and as such broke the drug code. He was returning to the team and if he was guilty of anything, it was of vanity. Over dinner with his parents, his Mum had an off-the-cuff swipe at him about his double chin. For someone who has been through the wringer in his time, Shane still remains and always will be a sensitive person. He hates to be made to look the fool, or for people to get the wrong impression about him.

He is the first to admit he has made some mistakes in his time, but when events are distorted or falsely reported or twisted in the media, which has been the case on a number of occasions, it really annoys him.

His life has become very public, and unless you have lived that life, you can have no idea how hard that is. I have tried to understand as his friend and done my best to support him through his difficult times, but at the end of the day, the loss of privacy really is a nightmare for him and his family.

I've been with Warney when he was on top of the world as the great Shane Warne, Australia's leg-spinning genius, but I have also been alongside him when he has been at the bottom of the barrel, down and out. The 12-month ban hurt him more than people really understood, but to his credit he kept a brave face and his public persona never really changed. Believe me, he was hurting really badly.

I honestly don't think he knew how big, bad and ugly the whole drugs thing was going to be. He called me from South Africa just before he faced the world's media and I have never heard him so low. I was worried about him as I turned on the television to watch him read from a prepared statement on the Sky news service. We spoke a lot during the next few days until he returned home, and I spent as much time as I could with him as he waited on the length of the ban to be decided.

A few late nights with his favourite ham and pineapple pizza were spent at his house as the media set up camp out the front, back and side of his home. The treatment he and his family received during this period of his life was disgraceful, more akin to something you might dish out to a criminal. In my opinion for cameras to follow his eldest daughter Brooke, then 5, to school was well and truly over the mark of decency. This really got to Warney. He just could not comprehend why his family had to be dragged into it, and I totally agreed with him.

The ban of 12 months was harsh, although I wasn't that surprised, especially once the World Anti-Doping Authority head Dick Pound and company weighed into the debate. In my opinion six months out of the game was what I thought his mistake deserved, but that's a point that could be debated forever. He broke the rules and needed to be punished, but in my honest view, the sentence outweighed the crime. I have no doubt that Warney's breach of the code was inadvertent, not deliberate.

During the ban, I often wondered how my friend was coping and we talked about it on a few occasions. The answer in short was that he was missing the competition more than anything. The thing that hurts elite athletes the most is not being able to compete. Injury has kept him off the field a few times during his career but to be injury-free and still not allowed to play or train must have been tough.

I distinctly remember hearing from him one night during the Australian tour of the West Indies partway through his ban. It was the fourth Test at Antigua when the Aussies needed four wickets on the final morning to win, and the Windies needed 47 runs. I was at home in my lounge room watching on Fox Sports when my mobile phone beeped indicating a text message had arrived. It was well after midnight and I wondered who would be texting this late at night.

The message read: "I'm really missing it now mate." That summed up Warney best of all. The Australians needed him, and he certainly needed them. The heat of battle got to him and he so desperately wanted to be there. As it turned out, Stuart MacGill was smashed by Vasbert Drakes and Omari Banks and the Windies won the Test, and Warney could do nothing about it in his lounge room, banned from doing what he loves most of all, competing when the heat is really on.

* * *

Although our careers began at roughly the same time, Warney has outstayed me. I suppose we both always hoped that we would play a Test match for our country together, and at the time of writing this book the series against India is in full swing, between us we have played 114 Tests! I unfortunately never fulfilled my childhood dream of a Test match, but my mate has more than made up for my absence.

He has just broken the world record going past Muttiah Muralidaran as the greatest wicket-taker in the history of the game, a monumental achievement. I must admit, with all his ups and downs, I didn't think he would climb so high, but once again, that's Warney. He has proven many people wrong throughout his career and I salute him for his perseverance.

During the 2002-03 one-day series in Australia, Warney suffered a career-threatening injury at the MCG one evening when he dived to stop a ball from his own bowling, dislocated his shoulder and did some serious ligament damage that required surgery. It was expected to keep him out of the game for at least six weeks, putting his place in the team for the upcoming World Cup in South Africa in jeopardy.

That night something very funny took place that must be recorded, even if it is slightly embarrassing. I was at the game hosting a corporate function upstairs in the Great Southern Stand when my friend went down with the injury, and being a little concerned, I excused myself and went down to the dressing rooms to see if he was okay.

The next thing I knew, I was stripping my suit off and getting dressed in the green and gold colours to act as 12th man, as Warney was clearly finished for the evening. Now understand two things at this point: I had waited 15 years for my chance to play for Australia, but also that I had been drinking through most of the match. If the truth be known, I would have been over the legal limit to drive, which was also over the limit to act as 12th man by some considerable distance.

But I figured that I would only need to take the drinks out, so it would not be a problem. Then as soon as I moved to the players' dug-out and Brett Lee spotted me acting as 12th man, he decided that he needed to go to the toilet. My heart-rate jumped from 80 to 180 in a matter of seconds. All of a sudden I was in the middle of the MCG in front of 60,000 people about to field for my country against the old enemy England, and I was half-cut.

Captain Ricky Ponting asked me to field at first slip to Jason Gillespie's bowling, to which I quickly replied: "I don't think that's a good idea, Punter. I'm half-pissed!" The look on his face was priceless, while the rest of the lads broke up laughing. In the end, I fielded two overs at long-off and thank God, I didn't have to field a single ball.

Thanks Warney. You always did say that you'd get me a game for Australia.

* * *

As Shane's career reaches its twilight stages, I start to think what he may do with himself when he retires. At 35 years of age, who knows how much longer he has left in the game? Perhaps the Ashes tour next year may be his swansong? I think a lot depends on the development of a replacement. If a young spinner steps up and is ready to take his place, I reckon Warney would give it away as he now has three wonderful kids who have grown up for most of their childhood missing their Dad. He has climbed every mountain there is to climb in the cricket world and been part of one of the best cricket teams in the history of the game.

Retirement is a word we never really spoke about much as both of us just love the game and figured we could play forever. The reality is that the emotional and physical strain takes its toll after so long at the top, and everyone eventually comes to the end of the road. Warney recently set up the Shane Warne Foundation, which is something he has wanted to do for a long time. He felt it was time to give something back to the world and his foundation's events will raise much-needed funds for various charities, all with the same theme of assisting children.

While he may be known by the public for making some poor errors in judgement in his life the Shane Warne I know has always been a loyal friend to me and my wife. He has a kind heart and has helped many needy people behind the scenes, a fact that has never been reported. Unfortunately only bad news sells newspapers. He has lived life full of the highest of highs and the lowest of lows and I'm sure there are still a few more to come before the journey is over. The thing that I most admire about him is his courage. To soldier on the way he has and to overcome the adversity he has faced has been unbelievable and to be totally honest, quite inspirational.

When the lights go down on his wonderful career, whenever that may be, I know we will play plenty of golf together, share a few beers while watching our beloved Saints, and share plenty of time with our families. It's a time I look forward to immensely as Warney and I will continue on in life as we have always been. As good mates.

CHAPTER 12 THE DYING ART OF WICKETKEEPING

The precious, old art of wicketkeeping is dying, and it hurts me to say that it's so. It doesn't have to be so. I hope it won't continue to be so. But I turn on the television and see Rahul Dravid keeping in one-day matches for India in his short sleeves, and I know that it's so. You don't keep in short sleeves because if you do, and you're playing on the subcontinent's sometimes grassless outfields, you'll take the skin off your elbows rolling for a catch. Dravid can't keep and even he knows it. Otherwise, he'd wear long sleeves like a real keeper.

I blame one-day cricket for this. In one-day cricket, wickets don't count for so much. It's all about making a bigger score than your opposition. In that environment, teams are looking for more ways to find extra batters and blokes who can hit. They sacrifice the keeper and stand a bloke behind the stumps who can whack a quick 50 with the bat. Then if it works in one-day cricket, some bright spark thinks they might get away with it in traditional cricket. Suddenly they don't want the keeper-batsman anymore; they want the batsman-keeper. It's a subtle difference, but it's killing the art.

Next thing you know, Alec Stewart is keeping for England for a decade or so and Jack Russell, one of the finest glovemen I've seen, is sitting behind him in the queue. Now Stewart couldn't keep beer cold. I've seen better keepers in a zoo. Technically, he was terrible. He'd drop to his knees, spill balls that should have been regulation takes. But here's the rub. Stewart was a competitor and a fine batsman. Result: he played 133 Tests for England and Jack Russell played 54.

Australians are not immune from this thinking. Partly, it's because we have not produced any high-quality all-rounders in recent years, blokes who could win their place either with bat or ball. This has put pressure on the wicketkeeper to provide extra support as a batsman, and it started with Wayne Phillips in the 1980s. David Hookes used to take the piss out of Phillips when he donned the gloves as an afterthought during that period. Hookesy and Ray Bright, the Victorian who played Tests and toured at that time, told me that Phillips did not even want to keep for Australia. He knew he couldn't keep. But they made him the keeper because he could bat, because he could slog them, like a poor man's Adam Gilchrist. That thinking still exists, too. Australia took Queenslander Jimmy Maher away on tour recently as a back-up keeper. Maher's a fine left-handed batsman and a good fieldsman. But a keeper? No way.

Australia's current wicketkeeper, Gilchrist, is a genius. There's no doubt about that. He changes games and wins games with his batting. But he is not a natural keeper. The ball doesn't disappear into his gloves like it went into Jack Russell's gloves or Ian Healy's gloves. I would suggest Gilly misses a chance in most Test matches. They're not necessarily visible to the untrained eye, but they happen. It might be a leg-side stumping, or a difficult catch, but it's all forgotten when he smashes a century with the bat, and the powerful Australian side walk away with a win.

Would I pick Gilchrist? Yes, I would, because he's a wonderful cricketer. I'd pick him as a batsman and play him in the top six, then select the best keeper after that. He wouldn't be my Test match wicketkeeper. I read recently that Richie Benaud had named Gilchrist in his all-time best team at No. 8 and as the keeper, and I find that surprising. I respect Richie but I can't believe that Gilchrist would go into his team ahead of Alan Knott, the great English wicketkeeper, or ahead of Ian Healy, the best Australian gloveman I've seen, let alone someone like Don Tallon from yesteryear, who Sir Donald Bradman selected in his greatest-ever Australian test team. Sure, pick Gilchrist at No. 6 in that team if you think he's good enough; but then have a Knott or a Healy as the keeper.

As you can see, I'm a purest, and I just don't understand that thinking. Growing up, my idol was Rod Marsh. I loved the way he launched himself to take those catches standing back to Dennis Lillee and Jeff Thomson. I read every book I could get my hands on: Alan Knott's, Marsh's, the Englishman Bob Taylor's. I watched videos prepared by Knott that I still have at home. But I soon found that it was a neglected art. I never had any real coaching. I was left to my own devices at training like all keepers are. It's neglected and it's being killed off.

My concern about this thinking is for the future. Who will be the role models for the new batch of young keepers, if teams are to use backstops rather than real keepers? Why would a kid put in the time and effort? Why not just go and learn how to bat? As a boy, I spent hours practising my stumping with the sweeping action. Right now, I wonder why any kid would bother.

My argument goes further. Stuart MacGill and Glenn McGrath are regularly picked to play Test cricket for Australia but let's be honest, they simply can't bat. Yet good bowlers are not questioned about this? They are specialists. Why does the wicketkeeper need to be a gun batsman, up at No. 7 in the order? Let's say you have a specialist wicketkeeper who stumps Brian Lara down the leg-side off Steve Waugh's bowling for 6, instead of Lara making 280. If you have a second-rate keeper behind the stumps and he misses the chance, he has to make 274 to make up for that. I've always believed that the keeper ought to be able to bat at eight or nine if that's where he belongs. He's a specialist, just like a bowler.

I realise I'm in the minority with this thinking but I wish people would consider it. I wish that they'd remember that Jack Russell won a couple of titles for Gloucestershire by standing up to the stumps to the quicker bowlers, creating the pressure, keeping the batsmen in their crease. Good keepers can do that. Backstops can't.

* * *

I believe that good keepers are born and not made. This is not to say that there is no requirement for hard work; the contrary would be true. I've never seen a good keeper who didn't have a decent work ethic. But it is a specialised skill and I'm not convinced that you can manufacture it.

The best Australian keepers I've seen are Ian Healy, Rod Marsh and Peter Anderson. Marsh was my hero when I was a kid, and then when I went to the academy in Adelaide, I saw Anderson at close range and loved his work. Anderson was an Alan Knott clone, right down to the old hat turned up at the front. He caught the ball "deep", by which I mean the way the ball went into his gloves. The coaches will tell young keepers to catch the ball down at the base of the index and middle fingers, but he caught it further down. The ball just disappeared so softly into his gloves.

Later on, I watched Healy up close, especially on the 1997 Ashes tour of England when his keeping to Shane Warne with the ball spinning and flying out of big footmarks was exceptional. Healy to me is the best Australian keeper, a guy who worked very hard to get better and ultimately became exceptional.

Not many non-wicketkeepers can tell the difference, but within the fraternity, we talk about it. I know that Mark Atkinson, who kept for a long time in Tasmania, was an outstanding gloveman. Wade Seccombe of Queensland was a beautiful catcher standing back, a little like Jeff Dujon, the great West Indian whom I loved to watch when I was a boy. Seccombe had that athleticism and he gave us plenty of grief catching nicks off the bowling of Andy Bichel, Michael Kasprowicz and company up at the Gabba over the years. Nick it anywhere from leg-slip to second slip and he'd catch it. Occasionally he'd come up to the stumps to, say, Adam Dale's bowling, but I never felt threatened by that. He wasn't great up to the stumps, but again, it's about opportunity and circumstance.

English keepers are generally better than Australians standing up to the stumps, I reckon, but they are not so good standing back. They don't use their feet and instead rely on hand-eye coordination. On Australian pitches, where the ball flies, this is a disaster. In Australia, you need to use your feet when you're standing back. Otherwise you can't cover the ground.

As I said, I'm not convinced that you can create a good keeper. To be a good wicketkeeper, you need to have a passion for the art. At training, you will be left on your own. You won't get much coaching or worthwhile advice. You have to be self-motivated. You will know that there is only one in every side, meaning that you have to be the best to secure a game. The best six batsmen will play and the best four bowlers. But to be the keeper, you need to be the best available and this can be frustrating.

In 15 years of first class cricket I was only a step away from the baggy, green cap of Australia. But in those 15 years, there was only one Test match in which neither Ian Healy, nor his successor Adam Gilchrist, were available to play. It was in Pakistan in 1994-95 and Healy had broken a thumb. Shane Warne rang me and told me that they would be calling in a replacement and that it was between me and Phil Emery, the New South Wales keeper. I was shattered when I saw on television that they had drafted in Emery, whom I'd played plenty of cricket against at national level. I was so close, but that's how tough the game is. Phil Emery extracted one Test match and a single one-day international for his years of grinding practice under the New South Wales coach and former Test keeper Steve Rixon. But it was one Test more than I played.

As the keeper, you're largely judged on your mistakes. Ian Healy referred to himself as "the drummer in the band", and it's a fair description. If the drummer belts away without a mistake, then he's not really noticed. If he hits the wrong drum at the wrong time, everyone notices. As a keeper, it's the same. You can have a good day for five hours and 50 minutes and then you make one error late in the day and that is what will be debated in the media that night.

I think some of the coaching that is done for keepers is too technical. I cringe when I have kids coming up to me and saying: "Should I take it on the inside of my body?" My answer is that you need to adopt your own style. I encourage kids to do that. I don't want them to try to be Ian Healy or someone else. You need your own flair and style.

Standing up to the stumps, I coach kids to forget about their feet. To me, standing up is mostly about hand-eye coordination and watching the ball very closely. Standing back, it's about footwork and concentration. There's that word again:

What an honour and a privilege to be part of the Ashes Tour of 1997.
'Tugga' and I at the London Bridge for the team photo.

From the paddock to the Baggy Green – my dream comes true.

Me with my childhood hero Rod Marsh during a
representative game against a touring Indian team.

Victory in Perth. Warney and I rarely sat this close
due to his bad habit of putting ash on my gear.

*An inspiration. I coached my little buddy Thomas Keefe
right up until his death in 1998 from Leukemia.*

Mercantile Mutual Cup celebrations 1994/95 versus South Australia.

Mercantile Mutual Cup win 1998/99 versus New South Wales.

Happy times during a house warming party in 1997.
L-R: Dennis Vague, John Scholes, Merv Hughes, me and Tony Dodemaide.

"Underneath the Southern Cross I Stand!" – Ian Healy leads the team with the
Victory Song after the Ashes were secured at Trent Bridge in 1997.

Merv at his brilliant best – spoiling a photo of the Warnes and the Berrys.

Mark Waugh stumped down the leg side off Cameron White. MCG 2003.

© Gary Sparke

Scoring a century against NSW at the SCG with Jon Moss. I'm about to kiss my mum's wedding ring which I wore around my neck after her death.

© Gary Sparke

The famous Ponsford stand at the MCG tumbles to the ground ... and so do I.

© Gary Sparke

Great leg-side catch: Cameron White at first slip, Bellerive Oval, Hobart.

concentration. A keeper needs to learn how to concentrate all day, or more specifically, at the right time.

The first problem that new keepers have is leg-side takes, and the notion of a leg-side stumping is fanciful to them. A lot of coaches in Australia will say: "Get yourself over early, as soon as you see it going down the leg-side." I disagree with this. As soon as you go early, you lose the ball momentarily and from there, you're guessing.

Going early, you lose the ball behind the batsman and you're guessing the length, and by extension the height. A lot of keepers bobble the ball in those circumstances. I watched the English keepers and they went late, as late as possible. The difference is that the extra instant of time allows you to pick where the ball is pitching and you get some idea of where to have your gloves in terms of height. Then at the last minute it's: "Go, take, sweep!"

I went to the AIS centre of excellence (formerly the academy) in Brisbane recently to do some coaching and when I told the young glovemen this, one of the coaches said: "But Ian Healy didn't do that!" My answer was that just because Ian Healy went early, that doesn't make it right. I'm saying that going late worked for me and that's what made me a good leg-side stumper. Once again, it's about what works for you.

I was a better keeper up to the stumps than standing back, I would say. Although at one point of my career I had grey gloves and Dean Jones and Matthew Elliott, the slip fieldsmen, used to say: "The grey nurse sharks are in the area. We won't get much today!" This was in reference to my diving in front of the slips to take catches. As a keeper you have your days. All sorts of little difficulties crop up over time. For instance, left-arm fast bowlers made it tough to cover the ground on a quickish wicket or a seaming strip. Tom Moody, the big Western Australian batsman, used to lift his bat up high in his stance and it blocked my eye line when up to the stumps. I spent two years trying to combat this, eventually moving way over to the off-side so that I could focus and get an uninterrupted view of the ball.

One issue that a young keeper needs to sort out could be categorised under: "When to go and when not to go?" A gloveman needs to know when to dive for the catch in front of or near the first-slip fieldsman and he can't afford to equivocate about it, otherwise he is going to put off the fieldsman or miss the catch himself. Early in my career I had problems with Simon O'Donnell, a poor slipper, when he was at first. I messed him up a couple of times and later Gary Watts came in there and we had the same problem. I thought about it, and from then on, I took the attitude that if I could reach it, I'd go. That's the advice I give to youngsters. You're in trouble if you start second-guessing. You need to get it ingrained that if it's in your zone, you go. I used to measure out how far I could reach at practice and my catching zone was two full steps. I'd mark that out, and that's where I would ask the first-slip fieldsman to plant his left foot. In 15 years, I reckon only a couple catches at most went between me and the first-slip fieldsman because whoever it was, he knew that it if it was in my zone, I was going for it.

How much practice does a keeper need to do? Wicketkeeping is a bit like golf, in that there's a lot of rhythm to it. It's a feel thing. Some days at training I'd catch for an hour; other days I'd do 10 minutes and feel right. If it wasn't right, I might stay for ages. But as a keeper your game is catching the ball. You need to repeat it day after day, year after year. When they practise for park cricket, they'll have the keeper out in the middle catching throws from the outfield. This is useless. A keeper needs to get in behind the batsmen in the nets and he needs to do it often, simulating what happens during a game. I also did a lot of yoga and boxing for the flexibility you need to stand behind the stumps, as well as squash and racquetball, games which approximated the footwork and skills required.

Early in my career at Fitzroy-Doncaster I would do hours of practice for leg-side stumpings, the toughest gig for a keeper. When everyone else went home, me and another keeper would grab someone's 'coffin' (hard-cased cricket bag), stand it up in the crease to represent the batsman, and practise that sweeping action. The reward for a wicketkeeper is when he makes one of those stumpings, or a diving catch, in a big game. As I have said, this is the moment when a keeper can change a game.

Fear is an important issue and it's true that it can be a dangerous occupation. I lost a tooth on a soft wicket in England in 1992 and from then on wore a mouthguard when I kept up to the stumps. That was unusual in my time, but it's definitely worth doing. My attitude was that prevention beat the hell out of cure. In my last two years, I wore a baseball-style face mask and I recommend that to all young keepers who are going to stand up to the stumps, especially on an uneven pitch. Once again prevention of injury is the aim, and if it helps a young keeper with confidence, all the better.

I've never been scared while I was keeping, but one day at the MCG Ian Harvey bowled a ball that took off from a good length and went straight over my shoulder without me seeing it, and it was soon after that I started to use the face mask. You can tell if a wicketkeeper is scared and it's not a good look. A keeper needs to be able to get up to the stumps and create the chances, build the pressure on a batsman. It won't happen if he's not comfortable being up there.

A lot of keepers over the years have used unusual and even bizarre methods of protecting their hands, in some cases lodging pieces of meat along their digits for instance, but I only used one method, and that was taping the joints. When I was playing for the Victorian under 16s in Perth early in my career the great Rod Marsh came in to talk to me and he showed me what he did. From then on I used eight centimetres of stretchy Elastoplast tape on every joint on every finger, every time I went out to keep. Some keepers tape a sore finger. I always taped every finger.

I wore one basic pair of padded inners and traditional gloves – the modern, one-day gloves to me are like gardening gloves — and although I dislocated fingers a few times, I had never missed a game in my career because of a hand injury of any sort until my final season in 2003-04. A ball smashed into the end of my middle finger on the left hand and broke it. I knew I was in trouble as soon as I took the next couple of balls and I was even more certain when I put my finger in ice at the end of the day. When you have broken a finger, the nerve ends are exposed and putting it in ice will make you go through the roof. That injury put a dampener on my last season.

"It's not the ones you take, it's the ones you miss," said my childhood mentor Bert Matcott and his words are true to this day. Breaks in concentration are the keeper's worst enemy and in that way, I think it is the toughest job in cricket. A fast bowler delivers six balls, then disappears to fine leg for a snooze. A keeper goes to sleep late in a day and that might be the one that is nicked low to the right and missed. I learned early in my career at the AIS in Adelaide that I couldn't expect to concentrate for a full six or seven hours. Therefore I went into relaxation mode between balls, talking to the guys in the slips cordon about anything and everything, not necessarily cricket. Once the bowler turned at the top of his mark, I'd stop chatting and switch on. Thirty-second bursts of concentration are what you want. You switch on, and then switch off.

Wicketkeeping is a tough task, and thankless a lot of the time. Try keeping to Merv Hughes in a feisty mood in Perth as I did one day, standing at least 30 metres back from the stumps and still taking the ball above my head every time, after flying above the shoulder of Mike Veletta, Western Australia's gutsy opener. Or in England in 1993, when I played for a World XI where the bowling attack included the South African Allan Donald, Courtney Walsh and Malcolm Marshall of the West Indies and the Kiwi Danny Morrison. Donald, the famed 'White Lightning' was as quick that day as anything I've seen or kept to. Then again I think the toughest day I put in behind the stumps might have been a Sheffield Shield match against a full-strength New South Wales in Sydney when Mark Waugh ground out a superb century against Shane Warne at his best. Warne, by some margin the best bowler I kept to, went around the wicket and bowled into the rough, trying to test the patience of Waugh. I recall being absolutely spent at the end of that day, probably the best day's state cricket I participated in, and a hell of a lot of fun as well.

CHAPTER 13 HEARTBREAK, RECORDS, INJURIES, LIFE AND DEATH

When Stuart Law came to Melbourne to play in the Pura Cup final of 2003-04, he said that he felt "about as popular as Osama Bin Laden" in Victoria. To which I was asked to respond soon afterward. "We prefer to think of him as Saddam Hussain," I said. "He's the one who got caught."

It is part of cricket folklore that twice in consecutive seasons, 1999-2000 and 2000-01, Victoria went to Pura Cup finals in Brisbane trying to break our hoodoo in that part of the world and twice came away empty-handed, and twice we departed with an image of the abrasive Law in our heads.

In the first of these games, Victoria versus Queensland in the 1999-2000 Pura Cup final at Allan Border Field, we were largely outplayed by the Bulls. But there was one window of opportunity for us and it involved Law, my old AIS academy mate. The Queenslanders were 5/111 and about 5/190 when we took the second new-ball. Law, on 76, nicked Mathew Inness to me behind the stumps and I swear it was such a big deviation that I took it near first slip. It wasn't a feather. He smashed it.

We went up, but umpire Steve Davis gave it not-out. The umpire would later say that he believed the deviation had come from Law's back leg. Queensland's captain went on to make 129 of their 285 when, had he been given out, they would have struggled to extract 220. Normally we wouldn't have expected Law to walk. But he'd hit the cover off the ball and that made it tough to stomach.

After that, Andrew Bichel destroyed us taking 6 for 47 in our first innings and realistically, I think we walked away feeling that it was a bonus to get to the final. I don't think we were ready to win; in the end, we drew a rain-effected final and Queensland took the championship as the top-of-the-table team.

But a year later we'd suffer a similar fate and this time, we were hurting more. Once again, the controversy involved Law. Again Queensland was the favourite, and we began with a moderate 176. Then we knocked them over for 242 and with a stronger second dig of 289 (Elliott 98, myself 61), we set Queensland 224 to take the crown again. It was game-on.

When the last day came around they needed just 87 with seven wickets in hand, and were on top. But we got a couple of early scalps and then when Law faced his first ball, he slashed Paul Reiffel toward Michael Klinger at third slip. Klinger dived and scooped it up, but Law would not go. "Did you catch that?" he asked Klinger.

Klinger, at that point a young and inexperienced player, replied that he had. But Law was not satisfied. The umpires conferred, and it went to the third umpire, Peter Parker, in the television box. As is so often the case when technology is called in, the replays were inconclusive. Law stayed.

The ensuing 15 minutes were the most hostile of any game I ever played. Law was under siege from 11 Victorian players who felt aggrieved, and that Law had questioned the sportsmanship of Klinger, a young player who had not a single devious bone in his body. Our captain, Paul Reiffel, was reported for dissent.

The incident was a big moment in Victorian cricket history. But the tale hadn't been completed. When he was 4, Law cut at Reiffel and nicked it to me behind the stumps, only to find that umpire Simon Taufel was signalling a no-ball. At 10, Matthew Elliott dropped him in the cordon. Law didn't need any more opportunities. He compiled an unbeaten 47 to get Queensland home by four wickets for another national championship.

I've never seen a more devastated bunch of players in a dressing room as that night. There were plenty of tears. A year earlier, we'd felt we had done well to reach the final. This time, we felt we could win it but that it had been taken away from us.

It's one of the reasons that, three years later, it felt nice to grind the Queenslanders into the dirt at the MCG when we batted for three days in the 2003-04 final. As a friend's message said on that day, it's called: "Redemption."

* * *

As I've recorded before, sport can be some sort of journey. Every elite athlete's worst nightmare is a serious injury, and I have to say that I've been lucky in that way. I look at my hands and they're not too gnarled for a wicketkeeper. I have to thank Rod Marsh for passing on his method of taping my fingers for that.

What's not widely known is that I almost missed the second of those Pura Cup finals against Queensland after I damaged the AC joint in my left shoulder in the second-last game of the season against New South Wales in Sydney.

I knew that I was in trouble from the moment Mick Lewis tackled me in a game of touch footy in the warm-ups in Sydney.

But not for one minute was I about to let on. I missed the last Pura Cup game against Western Australia and back in Melbourne, I was required to complete a fitness test that Steve Sandor, our physiotherapist, equated with the infamous test inflicted on Michael Malthouse by the Richmond coach Francis Bourke before the 1982 AFL Grand Final, also with a shoulder injury.

Sandor, who'd worked as a physiotherapist at Richmond in those times, had seen me in the dressing rooms the day I sustained the injury. We quietly slipped upstairs into the old umpires' room out of sight of my teammates and coaching staff. When I got my shirt off, rather painfully, 'Sad Sack' Sandor just looked and said: "Shit."

"Just tape it up and don't tell 'Barrel' (Scholes)," I said to him. Our physio wasn't happy with this. "Just do it," I said. We had a good relationship and a trust that had been built up over many years. I fielded that last day and couldn't lift my arm higher than my chest. All returns were taken in one glove when they came in high.

I'd spent a boring week in the hyperbaric chamber getting over the injury, but coach Scholes wasn't convinced. He must have hit 100 catches to me from all angles during that fitness test. Scholes wanted me to land on the shoulder; I was determined to protect myself. Eventually he relented. We walked out off the MCG nets and Barrel said: "What's it going to be like when the injections wear off?" This was funny, since I'd considered taking a painkiller but ultimately had not done it. I played the game, of course, and I'd have kept playing even if I'd popped the shoulder.

In my last year I missed seven weeks because of surgery on a finger, but outside of that I missed three or four games with injury in 15 years. When I watch the AFL and see the agony of a

Josh Francou or a David Schwarze, with multiple knee reconstructions, I know I'm very, very lucky.

* * *

As far as stats and records go to my way of thinking, my greatest achievement was playing in four title-winning teams for Victoria over 14 years. (2 Sheffield Shield/Pura Cup wins and 2 One day titles) They're the stats that matter most to me.

But it's a fact that along the way I accumulated some numbers that are worth savouring and I guess it is only now that I can look back upon them with some sort of pride.

I played more first class games for Victoria (138) than anyone, overtaking Dean Jones in my second-last season. I also played more Sheffield Shield-Pura Cup games (129) for Victoria than anyone else, and more domestic one-day matches (87) than anyone in Australia.

It's nice to think that I was a survivor, especially when I look at the names who had big numbers of games for my state – Jones, Ian Redpath, Keith Stackpole, Bill Lawry, Tony Dodemaide, Ray Bright. But to be honest, it's not a record you want to have. I can't hide behind the fact that I achieved this record because I was not in the national team for any length of time.

Every wicketkeeping record for Victoria sits alongside my name: most dismissals in an innings (8), most in a match (11, twice), season (54 in 1999-2000) and career (534). There is also the world record for runs conceded without a bye being taken, a mark set in my first year with South Australia.

With the bat, there is the Victorian sixth-wicket record of 290 with Matthew Elliott. There is my 50 from 28 balls in a one-day match against New South Wales at North Sydney Oval, which at the time was the second fastest-ever in that form of the game in this country. I also managed to score four first class centuries, unbelievably all against New South Wales with a highest score of 166 not out. These are numbers that I cherish since so many people criticised my batting over the years.

I regarded the Victorian captaincy as the second-most important job in Australian cricket behind the national leadership, and I'm proud to think that in 27 first class matches under my captaincy, we won 14 games at a 52 percent win rate. In the post-war period, it's the best percentage of any Victorian skipper. I hope this is a reflection of the positive manner in which I endeavoured to lead the team.

* * *

I'd like a dollar for every time I waited for the national selectors to name a team and I thought I might be half a chance. The most obvious of these was in 1994, when they needed to find a replacement for the tour of Pakistan, and Phil Emery got the gig.

But what really irked me over my time is that there were always plenty of people ready to heap praise on my keeping, but when it came time for selection in, say, an Australia 'A' game, I'd always miss out.

I've sat back and watched the likes of Brad Haddin and Wade Seccombe and Emery and Mark Atkinson and Ryan Campbell all play those types of games and I don't really understand why I didn't get a chance.

I am convinced that Victorian players were disadvantaged when Jim Higgs dropped off the national selection panel in the mid-1990s. I'm not saying the selectors are biased. Just that they know the players in their own states better. I have no doubt when it comes to a crunch decision it's easier to go with the devil you know as opposed to the one you don't. It has hurt the likes of Brad

Hodge, David Saker and Mathew Inness during my time. We get leapfrogged too often and it annoys me.

* * *

Sport's ups and downs pale into insignificance against the death of a loved one, and that's the kind of experience that puts life into perspective for you. I'm not a religious person and as such, I suspect that I don't understand it, therefore I find it difficult to deal with. But I do know that death played a big part in my life.

As a boy, Doug Rumble's tragic death gave me a chance at cricket. I lost my father before I had turned 21, and never got to go to the pub with him or learn about his time in the war. I saw both my parents draw their last breaths when I was still a young man and I was devastated by it. All these years later, there's still hardly a day when I don't see or hear something that reminds me of my parents, and it's even harder when you have a child of your own and you know that your Mum and Dad can't be there to share the joy with you.

My mentor John Scholes died too young and then David Hookes, my coach, was killed in 2004, that rollercoaster year. But there were others, as well. Around 1995 I met a brave, young boy named Thomas Keefe, whom I was coaching in a group of kids at the Hawthorn indoor centre. Thomas was 9 and the hardest trier of any of that group. But he had leukaemia.

We became close and I'll never forget the phone call to say that he had died when he was just 12. I wore a black arm band that day during a state game in Adelaide as a mark of respect for my brave young friend. By this stage of my life I was realising that I had put too much importance on cricket; that the picture was so much bigger.

In early-April 2004, a close friend from Wonthaggi, Blair Hunter, went to bed and later told his wife that he was struggling to breathe. He died later that night at 34, leaving a wife and two young children. It was later revealed that he had a problem with one of the valves in his heart. I spoke at his funeral, which was very hard to do given the circumstances of recent times. It showed me once again how life is so precious and how easily it can be taken from us. I vowed from that day forward I would live the rest of my life based on three simple things: health, family and friends. At the end of the day we worry so much about things in life we cannot change or control when realistically, all that matters are these three things.

I've had too much practice at dealing with death, and unfortunately, it doesn't get any easier. To be honest, I've had enough of dealing with it.

CHAPTER 14 JOHN 'BARREL' SCHOLES

I knew of John 'Barrel' Scholes long before I met him. Anyone who followed Victorian cricket would have. He sat alongside names like Stackpole and Redpath as the Gods of the game in my eyes, and our paths would cross from the time I was a teenager.

Back then, my parents were driving me from Wonthaggi to Melbourne each week to practise with the VCA's Keith Stackpole junior squad, and Barrel was one of the coaches. He was also coach of a Victorian under 19 game in Shepparton in which I played, and he was involved in the Crusaders, a collection of past players and up-and-comers for which I sometimes played, run by the businessman and cricket-lover Swan Richards.

Richards at the time headed up Gray Nicolls in Melbourne, and they became my lifelong equipment sponsor and supplier. Scholes was a sales representative for Gray Nicolls.

When I came back from Adelaide in 1990 and returned to my club Fitzroy-Doncaster, Scholes had crossed over from his original club, Carlton, to act as captain-coach, and we would play on the same team for years. He became my mentor and my friend, especially after both my parents had passed away. Barrel was a father-figure to me; much more than a cricket coach.

Scholes had played league football for North Melbourne as a rover in the 1970s, then in the VFA. In cricket, he was captain of Victoria at 21 and played in a Shield-winning team. He was a legend and not only because of his tangible feats. Barrel had a plastic hip, bung knees and a set of bandy legs that you could drive a car through. He lived on painkillers and anti-inflammatory tablets to deal with the pain of years of football and cricket, popping Panadeine Fortes like they were Smarties. He walked like a crab, waddling along with this peculiar gait, and in his later years as coach of Victoria the boys would get a giggle out of asking him to kick the footy. Often he'd fall over trying to kick it, that's how bad his injuries and ailments were. Barrel was a warrior.

As a coach and captain he was old-school, hard, uncompromising, relentless and incredibly competitive. He set high standards for everyone under his care and he didn't suffer fools. He had a big role in developing me as the person I am. He taught me about the honour of wearing the Victorian cap, the importance of turning up in the right gear and looking like a cricketer.

Barrel's methods were legendary in themselves. At practice, you weren't allowed drinks. Needing fluid was considered to be a weakness. "What, you can't get through the session?" he'd say. "You'll go more than an hour on Saturday and you won't get a drink."

He would not allow anyone off the track once we started our two-hour sessions at Fitzroy-Doncaster, not even for a toilet stop. I remember him breaking this rule once, when Brendan Joyce, a fine batsman who I'd started with at the club, had a dramatic call of nature. "I've got to go," said Joyce. Scholes made him bring the dirty toilet paper back on to the training track to prove it. That's how far he went.

Barrel was particularly hard on the ones he thought could play, and a lot of this hardness had been passed down at Carlton from Stackpole and Barney Jones and before that, Bert Numa. One of his favourite days was in 1993-94 when we beat a Melbourne team loaded with seven state players in the District grand final at the Junction Oval. Barrel called Melbourne "the cravat-wearers" and us the "fish and chip-eaters". He thought they were born with the silver spoon and with the best facilities, while we were battling away in the northern suburbs. He didn't mind the old us-against-them theory. Fitzroy-Doncaster had not had much success, and he delivered it for them.

In 1996-97 he became state coach after the catastrophic season when Dean Jones lost the captaincy and Les Stillman, the coach of the previous six seasons, was moved on. Our relationship changed a little at that point, because prior to that we were basically teammates and friends. He distanced himself a little and I could understand that, in the circumstances. He didn't want to be seen as favouring me, particularly when I was returning to the team from exile, and particularly because of the media coverage of the great fall-out. He rode me pretty hard.

Scholes told us that we were a laughing stock in Australian cricket because of all the in-fighting, and that we had to win back the respect of the cricket community. He saw his job as fixing the disharmony first, so that the cricket would come back on track, and there was no doubt in his mind what had been wrong.

He also said that it might take some time, and he was right. The first year was difficult. In the second year I captained the side for a while, but Jones did not want to play under me and was surly. Barrel was annoyed that it was taking so long to find some camaraderie. He'd been around sport long enough to know full well that a happy team is a good team.

In his third season, 1998-99, the tide began to turn and in his fourth and fifth seasons, we made the Pura Cup finals. Both times we went to Brisbane to play Queensland, and both times we came away without the trophy. The first one was a bonus for us, but Barrel was devastated by the second one because we could have won it.

We had some awkward and difficult times, especially beyond the 1998-99 season when we just missed the Pura Cup final and won the one-day title. I captained the team for much of the season in Warne's absence, and at the end of the season, he rang and asked to see me. No frills for Barrel. We met at McDonalds in Yallambie, near my home.

Barrel said he felt that Warne was away from Victoria too often and that they would need to make a change. He told me that I had paid my dues and that I was ready to become the permanent captain. The difficulty with this, of course, was that I was close to Warne. So I told Scholes that I needed it to be done upfront. Initially, I said that I would ring Warne immediately. But Barrel said to sit on it for a while and let him make the phone call. "I'm just telling you that you'll be captain of Victoria next season," he said.

I was very honoured but I didn't have much time to celebrate. A few weeks later, Paul Reiffel retired from international cricket and immediately, there was some speculation in the media that with him returning to a more permanent place in the Victorian team, he may skipper the state. I rang Barrel to find out what was happening, and he told me that it was only media talk; that nothing had changed.

With hindsight, it's clear that something definitely *had* changed. Maybe Barrel was pressured from above, I don't know. But soon enough, Pistol and I were called into Cricket Victoria for interviews. I couldn't see the point. As far as I was concerned, I had the job and no one had told me any different.

I was doing teaching rounds at Ivanhoe Grammar School when Shaun Graf, the cricket operations manager, left me a message to call him, and by the time I rang him back at lunchtime, he said he needed to see me as soon as possible. It was urgent. Straight after school, we met at the Tower Hotel in Ivanhoe, and Graf told me that there would be a press conference at 5pm to announce that Paul Reiffel would be captain of Victoria. Graf wanted me there to talk at the press conference because I would be vice-captain.

It was like being hit between the eyes with a sledgehammer. I said: "Barrel told me that I was going to be captain." He said: "Sorry mate."

All this time down the track, I think about it and it is the process that concerns me rather than the actual decision. If someone had come to me earlier and told me that Pistol had become available, and that they had given it some thought and changed their mind, then I might have had a better chance of accepting it. I don't know what was happening in the background. But some warning would have been nice.

Ninety minutes later I was sitting in front of the cameras and microphones at the Cricket Victoria offices in Jolimont and putting on the brave face, saying all the right things. What I remember clearest is that Barrel couldn't make eye contact with me.

Technically as vice-captain I was in the same position as the previous season. Realistically, I had been vice-captain to Warne, who was away most of the time, and hence the surrogate captain. Under Reiffel, I would have no such responsibility. So it was effectively a demotion for me, and I figured my chance to captain the state had passed.

I fronted Barrel in my usual way and was given a few reasons as to why I had been overlooked for the captaincy. One of them was that Warnie and I kept wearing our hats backwards at practice, and that this showed a lack of leadership. Barrel hated it. Another was that I had shuffled the batting order in one-day matches the previous season, using pinch-hitters. Another was that I had pushed up too hard for Mick Lewis, my Northcote teammate and a fine fast bowler, at selection.

I couldn't accept that there were any legitimate reasons amongst them, and I can only conclude that with my strong personality, I had rubbed people the wrong way again. Barrel and I remained friends, but it was never quite the same after that. We spoke about it, without ever really finding any closure, which was a pity in the light of what happened later.

Barrel made me the person I am today, but when he had to deal with that person and work together with that person, our strong personalities sometimes clashed. As captain, I felt that he missed his involvement as a player deeply (remembering that he had only retired recently to take on the state coaching job). He'd always told me that the captain was the most important person in a cricket team, but when he became coach, he wanted more control. I had never forgotten what he'd said to me earlier in our careers about the skipper coming first. The reality is that in a coach-captain situation, Barrel worked better with Paul Reiffel than he did with me.

* * *

Johnny Scholes loved the Vics and would have been delighted with the result that the 2003-04 season delivered, finally bringing the Pura Cup back home after a long absence during the barren 1990s.

In both his last two seasons as coach of Victoria, we made the Pura Cup final, but couldn't quite manage to collect the silverware. He did an outstanding job, restoring respect within cricket circles towards our squad and I believe that our success had a lot of Barrel's work behind it.

But Barrel had a health problem that had emerged in his final season and I was one of the few who knew about it. Shaun Graf asked me about it in Brisbane one night, in what I thought was a frank discussion between two people who really cared about Barrel. I told Graf the honest truth, which was that I thought he was struggling with the demands of the job, due to the private health issues he was facing in his life. Somehow this found its way back to Barrel, who was annoyed.

I was deeply concerned about him, and had discussed this in private with my wife, but Barrel was an intensely proud man who always fixed other people's problems, but would not let you in to fix his. Sadly, he pushed me away at this time.

At the beginning of the 2001-02 season, Barrel resigned as coach, citing "private family reasons" for his decision. There is no doubt his health got the better of him and it effected his performance in the job. Mick O'Sullivan, who was chairman of selectors, took over for the season and put his heart and soul into the job. Unfortunately it was an ordinary year as far as results go, one in which Reiffel retired midway through the season.

David Hookes was hired to coach the team from 2002-03 and I lost a bit of touch with Barrel.

On my way to a pre-season training session at the Tan track on the 14th of July 2003, I got a phone call to say that he had suffered a heart attack and that it was serious. I finished my training session and by the time I turned my phone back on, there were a few messages. Barrel had died.

I was numb, but I rang Paul Reiffel, who thanked me for letting him know. Barrel and Pistol had been close. I walked down on to the bank of the Yarra River and I sat there for 20 minutes, crying with Mick O'Sullivan as we looked across at the lights of the MCG.

John Scholes and I were once very close friends, but had drifted apart towards the end, which to this day still upsets me, for I can honestly say I loved Barrel. His death rocked me like losing my parents had earlier in my life. I really missed the chats we used to have about life and cricket. I'll never forget what he taught me as a person and the impression he has left on my life.

Barrel was indestructible, I thought. I wished.

CHAPTER 15 VICTORIAN CRICKET: A BUMPY RIDE

Pulling the navy blue cap of Victoria over my head just once meant everything to me. To sit here 15 years later as the man who has played the most games for my state is an enormous thrill. I'm very proud of that. We had our highs and our lows over that journey, but my abiding memories, of course, are the four titles – the Sheffield Shield in 1990-91, the Pura Cup in 2003-04 and the two limited-overs championships in 1994-95 and 1998-99.

There was too wide a gap between the first and last titles, but that's a result of underachievement by Victoria. I have no doubt we could have – should have – done better. We were overtaken by Queensland and Western Australia and outperformed by New South Wales, and there are reasons for this.

In the early part of my career we were dogged by unrest and fierce personality clashes that stopped us performing as a unit. Mistakes were made in terms of appointments, too many good players were allowed to leave, others were poorly treated, and facilities provided for the players were not up to the mark. These things were a constant source of frustration for me over the 15 years.

LEADERSHIP

The Victorian cricket hierarchy always went for the big name and the bloke who would deliver the sponsor's dollar above the guy who could do the solid job. In my time, the captains of Victoria were Simon O'Donnell, Dean Jones, Shane Warne and Paul Reiffel, all international players and fine cricketers. But while he was an aggressive player, O'Donnell's captaincy record reflects a conservative approach, and we played too many draws. This was a falling out from the earlier period led by Ray Bright, when Victoria developed a reputation for dour cricket.

When O'Donnell fell out with the hierarchy and departed, Jones took over and immediately was more attacking in his approach. He was a breath of fresh air, but sadly, he had poor man-management skills. Despite his greatness as a player, the side fell apart under his captaincy. So we moved on to Warne, arguably this state's best-ever cricketer, and a very good captain in his own right. Tactically, Warne was the best I played under. But he was never there enough because of his international commitments. I've always favoured the Queensland model for leadership, where Stuart Law had the job and was there all the time, and I believe the state captain in Australian domestic cricket needs to be a regular state player.

When John Scholes and Cricket Victoria came to the same conclusion and replaced Warne, they chose Paul Reiffel, who had retired from international cricket and hence, was available to play and make the commitment to the state. He led by example rather than words, and he was outstanding in that sense during his first season. As his body began to let him down he struggled in his second year, and by the middle of his third season he had retired. Still, he took us to two Pura Cup finals.

I believe there were alternatives to the first part of the equation. Jamie Siddons left Victoria after we won the Shield in 1990-91 and went to South Australia, ultimately captaining that state to a Shield triumph. He would have been a wonderful skipper for Victoria. Because he wasn't being picked for Australia, he would have been around all the time. He was an aggressive captain and a great player. He wasn't a South Australian, he was a Victorian. And we lost him.

When Jones took over it fell apart and we suffered three years of infighting. But all the while we had the likes of Tony Dodemaide and Wayne Phillips in the ranks, good strong Victorian players who were role models for younger men. In cricket, leadership is important. It's about massaging players' egos, allowing them their freedom to express themselves within the constraints of a team environment.

But we went for the big names first and foremost, and it cost us.

MISTAKES

In Victoria over my time, we didn't always treat our players like we valued them. A succession of them left to join other states. A couple of them, Paul Jackson and Mark Ridgway, became very good players in their adopted states. Others like Adam Dale, Peter McIntyre, Simon Cook and Brad Williams departed and became Test cricketers representing other states.

Players swap states all the time. It's commonplace nowadays. But the two who stick in my craw are Siddons and David Saker. I've spoken about Siddons already. But when Saker went to Tasmania in 2000-01, I was gutted. I had pushed up for his selection a few years earlier and he had not let me down. We were great mates off the field. Saker had been in the state squad a few years prior to that, but was considered to be too much of a free spirit. He went back to club cricket and then had a second crack at the state team in the mid-1990s, quickly becoming one of the best fast bowlers in the country.

He was about 32 when Victoria let him go to Tasmania, which had offered him substantially more money and a two-year contract. When he sat down with Cricket Victoria, his ranking had slipped and the money wasn't there. It told him everything about where they thought he was at. He had little option but to move. But in my mind, he had a couple of years left, in which he could have helped the development of the younger bowlers.

I can think of at least two talented, young players who were not properly treated by Victoria. One was Craig Howard, the tall leg-spinner who at the time was the most gifted bowler of his type I had seen in my state. He had this vicious wrong 'un that a few batsmen could not pick (I stumped Siddons, one of the best players of spin I've seen, down the leg-side from this delivery one day).

But Howard was cast aside too early, played when he should not have played and then not persisted with when he should have been nurtured. Jones ran down the wicket smashing him in a club game and sledged him. I reckon he should be playing for Victoria still. But he's not even bowling leg-spin any more and he's dropped out of Premier cricket altogether.

One of the worst decisions I saw in my time was the declaration that left Michael Klinger stranded on 99 not out at Bellerive Oval in Tasmania in 2000. I believe that Klinger, a former Australian under 19 captain, was a confidence batsman. I'm not sure he ever got over this day. Certainly he has not arrived as the player we expected.

I was batting with Klinger and we were told there would be a declaration around 12.30. But when the time ticked over, captain Paul Reiffel did not call us in. Klinger was in his early 90s, so I assumed they were waiting for him to secure his maiden first class century. Fair enough, too. We pushed on for a couple of overs and when he was 99, I came on strike and let the last two balls of an over pass, so that he would have the chance to get the run he needed in the following over.

But Reiffel was standing on the stairs outside the dressing room and gesturing us to come in. The Tasmanian players were actually laughing about it out on the field. I put my hands out as though to say: "What's going on?" I probably shouldn't have done that, but I was furious. Klinger didn't say much, but I know he was shattered.

There was a lot of tension in the rooms, and Scholes said: "It's unfortunate but team comes first."

I agree with Scholes and I always played that way. But my objection is that no message came out from the rooms. If they were going to declare, then why not at the designated time? They let us go on, but then pulled the pin on Klinger when one more ball might have been enough.

It's always upset me that great Victorian players completed their careers with the state in an messy way. Merv Hughes was on the outer just as much as myself in 1995-96, and ultimately played out his career with a couple of seasons with Canberra Comets when they were briefly admitted to the national limited-overs competition. Dean Jones departed with scars. Simon O'Donnell fell out with Bill Lawry. Damien Fleming went and played with South Australia and ended up coaching at the AIS in Brisbane, lost to Victoria. David Saker went to Tasmania for security. It's part of the reason I retired when I did. I wanted to go out on my own terms, without scars, as I had devoted almost half of my life to Victorian cricket and it meant a lot to me.

NOMADS

When Simon O'Donnell and Dean Jones captained Victoria, they fought with the Victorian Cricket Association about the fact that we didn't have a home base. We were shuffled all over the place to train, and there's not a private school or an indoor centre in Melbourne that we haven't occupied at some stage.

But O'Donnell fell out with the management over his claims, and so did Jones. Ten years later I was having the same arguments. I told them: "This is a joke."

It *is* a joke. Cricket Victoria has been all over the shop with this. It poured money into the Junction Oval, got the nets up to scratch and made the rooms liveable so that it felt like home. At one point, Optus Oval in Carlton was the favoured venue. Then Punt Road Oval in Richmond was the chosen alternative venue to the MCG, and they spent money there to bring it up to first class standard. During this time the MCC had built a new gymnasium at the MCG adjacent to the nets, which we were allowed to use, but the grandstand was knocked down and replaced and with that went the gym.

Nowadays it is back to the Junction Oval again but the facilities are still not up to scratch. There's no indoor centre and no gym. There's no place where you walk in, see your locker and think: "I'm part of something special, here."

Don't get me wrong. I know these things cost money and I know that Cricket Victoria has a deal to play its games at the MCG whenever that's possible. But I don't think it's too much to ask that an alternate venue be set up properly. What this is about is having a home. I use the example of North Melbourne Football

Club, which operated out of basic facilities at Arden Street for years. The facilities weren't great, but at least they had a home.

All the other states have a home base. Queensland has done wonderfully well with the Allan Border Field, and has its gymnasium, nets and centre wicket practice available there; South Australia, New South Wales and Tasmania all have indoor facilities on site at their home ground where they train. Western Australia owns the WACA Ground and does everything there, albeit in just ordinary indoor facilities.

In 2003 I went to a meeting at Cricket Victoria and I took a list with me. I wanted to make a point with it. The list contained every single venue in Melbourne at which I'd trained over my 15 years. It contained something like 80 venues. I showed it to Tony Steele, a CV board member who was chairing the meeting. "Simon O'Donnell fell out with you guys for the same things I'm about to say," I told him. Steele said my points were valid but that CV had a long-term agreement with the Melbourne Cricket Club and that an alternative venue wasn't high on the agenda. I told him: "I just hope in 15 years' time Cameron White's not sitting here having the same argument."

So what's happening this season? Victoria is playing its first few games at the Junction Oval because of the MCG redevelopment, then back to the MCG after Christmas. Training is at the Junction, but the indoor facility which is privately owned and not by Cricket Victoria incidentally, was miles away adjacent to Monash University in Clayton. It has recently changed ownership and Cricket Victoria still pay externally to use a private facility as opposed to owning its own. Swimming will be at the Melbourne Sports and Aquatic Centre and the gymnasium they use is a public venue at a shopping centre in Richmond.

We are the nomads.

I think we need to take our state cricket away from the MCG, where there is always a chance we'll be kicked off for a concert or a bigger event. That's the commercial reality. We need a boutique venue like North Sydney or Allan Border Field where they can build a social club and put photos of our history around the walls. At the moment we're all over the place. And how can you build a culture and team morale out of that?

TENSION

In my time there was always a distance between the hierarchy of Cricket Victoria (formerly the VCA) and the players. They employed Bill Lawry as cricket manager and then the role of cricket operations manager was taken by Shaun Graf, who'd been a selector before that.

Graf is a former state and international player and a legend of club cricket in Melbourne. He was meant to be a conduit between the playing group and the board. But from the players' perspective, the message clearly does not get through. We had virtually no contact with the board itself, and so far as the players could see, the board had little idea of what was happening at the coalface.

Personally, I thought Graf ought to have been made accountable for some of the mistakes that have been made, as it would be in any big business where the buck stops at the top. He was a big part of some of those decisions.

The level of tension has always been high. I recall once that the Cricket Operations department handed out a questionnaire at the end of a season that was marked 'Strictly Confidential'. It was standard business practice. We were required to tick boxes to indicate how we thought certain aspects of the operation had gone, but controversially, we had to express opinions about the performance of the support staff, including the coach and administration, and the relationships between players and the board. Clearly it needed to be confidential.

But I got a call from Laurie Harper, a state squad member, who had picked up that there was a code on the bottom of the questionnaire which identified every player. The alarm bells were already ringing, because my wife Katherine, who works in the human resources field, had picked this up as well. The players were disturbed, because some of them had already returned the questionnaires to Cricket Victoria. Once again the tension rose, and the trust between players and the cricket operations manager hit rock bottom.

HOODOO

Regardless of some frustrating issues I need to highlight that I loved my time with Victoria. But one thing that I never did was to play in a winning first class team on the Gabba in Brisbane.

Our hoodoo at the Gabba was infamous in Australian cricket for years. We tended to go to play Queensland early in season and we were mostly under-prepared because of the Melbourne weather and the fact we didn't have our own indoor facility. We often went to Brisbane too defensive and negative, as well. I always believed we needed to pick batsmen who would play some shots, and dinky seam bowlers rather than trying to blast them out. We also needed a spinner, too. Shane Warne always loved playing there because the wicket bounced.

Our only outright win in my time came in the summer of 2003-04, and as it happened, I missed the game because of my broken finger. But I did manage to see the victory. I woke up in Melbourne on the morning of the final day with the boys about to undergo a run chase, and I jumped on a plane to Brisbane. I couldn't miss this moment.

Then when I got in a taxi at the other end I heard we'd lost a few wickets. I nearly turned around. I thought I was jinxing them. When I got to the Gabba, I couldn't make myself obvious, so I slipped into the Queensland Cricketers' Club and rang my old mate Michael Horan, from the *Herald Sun*. Horan had covered more of my career than anyone else, and I knew that he would have as good a feel for what this meant as anyone. I remember one year at the Gabba, he'd managed to momentarily stop a Sheffield Shield match because they'd put the journos in a box up on top of the Lions' social club, and the argument he was having on the phone was so loud that Allan Border stopped and turned around on the field. Both Border and Jones, standing at slip, knew Horan well. "Must be having a blue with his editor," said Border. Actually the argument was with his wife. We often have a laugh about that day.

I told Horan to meet me in the bar and we had a couple of beers as Victoria crossed the finish line. I went down to the rooms after Victoria won, and Wade Seccombe, the Queensland wicketkeeper, just laughed. "We've lost but at least you weren't part of it!" he said. Although I had not played in the game it was still a very proud moment after all the poundings we had copped over the years at the Gabba.

David Hookes couldn't understand why I would turn up. But Cameron White, who was captain in my absence, did understand. "I knew you'd be here," he said.

CHAPTER 16 **HOOKESY**

I went a long way back with David Hookes. He'd been my initial captain at first class level, and he gave me the opportunity when I was a kid at the academy in Adelaide. He treated me hard back then, but I respected him nevertheless. He was a phenomenal player and a formidable person. If he was tough on me at the start, then he helped make me the person I am. He had an influence on me, that's for sure.

When Hookes was appointed coach of Victoria in 2002 it raised a few eyebrows, including mine. By his own admission, Hooksey had stayed away from cricket dressing rooms since his retirement as a player a decade earlier. He'd been out of the loop for a few years. Plus so far as I could tell, he had always *hated* Victorian cricket. It was that old 'Kick a Vic' mentality and the parochialism that comes out of Adelaide toward Victoria, both in cricket and football.

All of a sudden he was our coach, and I was thinking: "This will be interesting." And interesting it was.

Hookes' appointment had been pushed by Shane Warne, by the cricket operations manager Shaun Graf and by Chairman Geoff Tamblyn, after Mick O'Sullivan did the job for a season following the death of John Scholes. Cricket Victoria had an interview process for the job, but it was window-dressing, in my view. Jamie Siddons and O'Sullivan were among those who had interviews, but Hookes, whose main gig was working as a broadcaster with Fox Sports and 3AW, got the job without ever doing one as far as I know. I reckon he was always getting the job.

Now Hookes could not run a training session to save himself. He was not a great coach in that way. What he was good at – and this is why he left such an impression – was getting people to believe in themselves. He was brilliant in that area. Hookes had Jonathon Moss, David Hussey and guys who had struggled to make an impact previously believing they were legends. They felt like they could do anything. He had Brad Hodge playing with freedom again whereas under Scholes, Hodgey seemed to be always worried about getting out, scared of making the mistake. Hookes got him to go out and play which was exactly what he needed to do.

Mechanically, Hookesy had very little idea, but he was smart enough to appoint Greg Shipperd as his assistant, another hiring that raised eyebrows. Shippy had coached Tasmania for 10 years and had a more traditional approach to the job. He ran training, and Hookesy did the big-picture stuff. It was a perfect combination, and I have to say that Cricket Victoria got it right.

In Hookes' first season, 2002-03, he showed himself to be a disciplinarian. He was old-school in that way but mainly, he did what he said he'd do. He was in your face. We got bowled out for 65 in a one-day match against Queensland at Ballarat and the coach ordered a week of 6.30 am swimming sessions in Port Phillip Bay. If anyone missed a session, they were to be suspended for two matches.

Deep down I thought he'd gone over the top with the swimming sessions for one bad performance. But I went along with it. Then on the fourth morning, I made a mistake with my alarm after coming home late from the Allan Border Medal presentation, slept in and missed the session. I phoned Hookes immediately and apologised. I met him later that day when there was a trial game at Scotch College. We walked a lap together and talked about it. "I can't go back on my word, mate," he said. We agreed I had to cop my medicine, even though I was shattered to give up my place, and embarrassed that I'd had to explain my simple human error – setting the alarm for 5.30pm instead of 5.30am — to the media.

Hookes had Warne back as captain of the team and Matthew Elliott as vice-captain, but after we lost the first Pura Cup match in Adelaide under Elliott's leadership – Warne was away with the national team – Elliott told Cricket Victoria that he wanted to step down and concentrate on playing his own game. Hookes asked me to be the stand-in captain when Warne was unavailable, but I declined initially. "What do you mean, 'no'? I thought you were supposed to be passionate about this?" he said.

I told him that I'd been burned by losing the job before and I didn't want to put myself in that position again. "Mate, I *need* you to do it," he said. So I agreed to stand in for the rest of that season, and we just missed the Pura Cup final, but were disappointing in the one-dayers.

At the beginning of Hookes' second year, the 2003-04 season, he told me he was looking to the future. "How much longer have you got?" he said. I told him that in all honesty, I hadn't even thought about retirement. Hookes told me that he was looking at Cameron White as a captain; that White could be captain of Australia one day and they needed to groom him. It was typical Hookes left-field thinking. The situation had been forced by the 12-month suspension of Shane Warne for breaking the drug code.

I said that pushing up White was a good idea, but I was concerned about Cameron's lack of experience. My worry was that White would be captaining a team that included Warne, Elliott, Ian Harvey, Brad Hodge and company, all players who had been around for much longer and achieved much more. John Scholes had drilled into me the notion that you earn your stripes in the game. White hadn't played enough, in my opinion.

"Not for one minute do I think that Cameron can't do it," I told Hookes. "I think he'll be an excellent captain. But he hasn't established himself. It's not fair on him. It's not like footy, where you're made captain and you can go out and crash bodies and inspire your teammates. In cricket, you have to massage personalities. At first class level, it's an off-field job as much as it is on-field."

We had a spirited debate about it and looking back, I think he was feeling the water with me. We ended up with a compromise position. White would captain the side in one-day games, and I would be captain for the Pura Cup matches.

Hookesy and I had healthy debates. But one thing about him, there was always a clean slate the next day. I liked that about him. Sometimes I would win; sometimes he would win. But it didn't carry over or get personal.

He could be a smart arse, too, and this anecdote shows how. One of our biggest disagreements in that season was over declaring our first innings closed in the game against Western Australia at the Junction Oval. I wanted to declare once we passed WA, so we could make a game of it, push for outright points. Hookes, Shipperd and O'Sullivan wanted to bat on for a while and build up a lead, and I was outvoted, so to speak. On the last day we were set a total to chase but rain intervened, and we ran out of time, and I went off my head about it. I was having problems of my own, because I'd played the game with a badly-injured finger and hadn't been able to catch properly with it. I knew then that I needed surgery that would keep me from playing for a while.

So off I went for my date with the surgeon, and Victoria ploughed on without me. They were in Perth a little later in the season and they knocked over WA for not many. This message turned up on my phone: "Chuck, it's Hookesy. I'm here with Spotty (Ray Bright, a selector). I know you're in Melbourne. Bad luck about that, mate. Listen, we've just passed WA and I was wondering if you'd like us to declare or not?"

I kept that message on my phone for ages. It was *so* David Hookes. It carried the sarcastic Hookes wit, and the underlying message that our falling out earlier in the season had passed. And by the way, we batted on and won that match.

Hookesy fitted my personality and I'd say we were fairly similar. We were both smart arses and had strong opinions, we would disagree about things, but then let it go. Life's too short to hang on to small differences or allowing things to get personal.

I admired him. He'd done a lot of things that I wanted to do in life. He'd called football, which was a passion of mine. He'd gone into the media which was where I felt like I was headed. He got me a job as a panellist with Inside Cricket on Fox Sports. He was a genius as a cricketer but I admired the fact that when he stopped, he made a career for himself as a broadcaster, and not necessarily only because he'd been a high-profile player. He was good at it.

As coach, he taught us that we could win from any situation. That was the mentality we took through that season and the famous run chase against New South Wales at Newcastle is the best example.

I didn't play that game; I was still recovering from the surgery on my finger. But I went to the match because Hookesy and I had needed to go to Sydney to shoot a program for Inside Cricket, and we drove the two hours up to Newcastle afterward. We talked a lot along the way, about things that I remember clearly in the light of what happened later in the season. I remember him talking about how he wanted a contract extension for a couple of years. We chatted about a lot of things.

Victoria ended up chasing 455 in just more than a day's cricket, on the surface an unrealistic target from 110 overs. Hookes masterminded the chase. He wouldn't have any talk of saving the game. He told us that it was like two, consecutive one-day games with 225 to win in each of them, and 55 overs to get the runs. Obviously he said we needed to keep some wickets in hand in the first of those segments. But he made the chase sound manageable all of a sudden. He wrote it up on the whiteboard and that night, the boys walked home believing it was possible. He told us that South Australia had chased 500 once and got them. He made them believe that they could pull off a miracle.

Stuart MacGill was in the New South Wales side and the wicket was spinning. But Victoria was on track at the halfway stage and David Hussey played one of the greatest innings I have seen, an amazing 212 not out. History records that Victoria won by three wickets with eight overs to spare.

Had John Scholes been coaching Victoria in that match, he would have told us that we needed to play for our pride, and not to give up our wickets to the New South Welshmen. Hookesy's attitude was: 'Let's try and win'. That's why he was so good. He had his 'For What It's Worth Basket', which was a little collection of anecdotes and sayings. He'd tell us a story and then say: "Put that one in the For What It's Worth Basket'. The one he told us at Newcastle was about the tennis at Wimbledon. "You can lose more games than you win, but still win Wimbledon," he said.

"You can lose 6-0, 6-0, then win 7-6, 7-6, 6-4 and you're the champion."

We used to take the piss out of him sometimes. When he arrived, I quickly dubbed he and his coaching staff the 'Sky Hookes' after the rock band of the 1970s, the implication being that they were, as the song goes, Livin' in the 70s. The coaching group (Hookes, Shipperd, Rodney Hogg, Ray Bright, John MacWhirter and Mick O'Sullivan) were all from that era.

Brad Hodge, a budding amateur comedian, copped a spray from Hookesy one time and quickly labelled the room at the MCG in which the coach had given him the barrage 'The Wrath Room'. We put a sign up to that effect soon afterward. He had this customary reply when you tried to tell him something: "Sure. Sure, understand." And he said it so much that the boys began mimicking him.

Hookesy had a hard exterior but he loved coaching the Vics, loved being involved in a team environment. My memories of that couple of years will be of him with a beer in his hand and laughing in the rooms. It wasn't easy to break through that hard exterior. But the night we beat New South Wales in Newcastle, he rang his mate Gerard Healy, his co-host on 3AW's Sports Tonight program, and he was like a little kid: "We've just pulled off the greatest chase you've ever seen!"

We stayed in the rooms for hours that night, and Hookesy decided we'd walk back to our hotel instead of taking the bus. It must have made a sight, this bunch of cricketers, well lubricated and most still in their whites walking along the side of the road. We found a corner pub, and I suggested we go in for a pot. The publican lined up pots on the bar and he was rapt, because news of our achievement had spread quickly. After we drank the beers, he asked if we had a memento that he could keep. Hookesy stripped the training shirt off his back right then and there, borrowed another one from Mick Lewis to put on, and we all signed the shirt and gave it to the publican. Hookesy wrote on that shirt: THE GREAT CHASE 2003-04.

A fortnight later, Hookesy would be dead.

* * *

Soon after the Newcastle game, we played a one-dayer against South Australia at the MCG. My hand was okay and I wanted to play, but Hookesy talked me out of it, saying that I should delay my return to the side until the four-day game that was to be played a few days later.

The Vics beat SA in the one-dayer, and Hookesy was rapt to beat his old mates, Wayne Phillips, the SA coach, and Darren Lehmann, the skipper. Generally after a win we adjourned to the London Tavern in Richmond, but for some reason we decided to change our routine on this night. We headed to the Beaconsfield Hotel in St Kilda, a decision that still haunts me.

There was a big crowd when Rob Cassell, Andrew Lynch, our former fitness adviser, and I arrived at the Beaconsfield, and there was a queue outside as there often was on a Sunday night. Hookes, who was on his way, rang and left a message on my mobile. "Tell the bouncers to make sure they let Lehmann and Phillips in. See you soon," he said.

We had an enjoyable few hours. There was a television in the bar and we were watching a one-day international, with Hookesy as ever sprouting opinions and criticising the way Michael Bevan was batting for Australia. Late in the night, Lynch and I decided that we needed food and we took a taxi to nearby Fitzroy Street. I hadn't seen anything that indicated there would be any trouble at the hotel.

A little while later I was in a taxi going home when one of the group rang me to say that Hookesy had been knocked out, and that it didn't look good. They were giving him mouth-to-mouth resuscitation, and Cassell and the SA physiotherapist, John Porter, were tending to him. I got the taxi to turn around, and headed back to St Kilda, concerned, but not necessarily fearing the worst at this point.

The ambulance had taken him away to hospital by the time I came back, so I headed straight to the Alfred Hospital. The looks on people's faces when I arrived told me how serious it was. Lehmann and Phillips were there. Shaun Graf, Shipperd and Cassell had gone to the police station to give statements. I was told that Hookesy had been involved in an exchange with one of the security staff outside the hotel, as he was about to get into a car in a side street near the hotel, and that he'd been knocked out. Worse, he'd hit his head on the road as he went down and they hadn't been able to revive him. My friends told me that it had all started with the lights coming on and the bouncers calling: "Last drinks." They said that a girlfriend of one of the players had passed comment to a bouncer, and there had been a short verbal exchange during which Hookesy spoke up on her behalf. They had all left the hotel, but the argument spilled outside. I was told that Hookesy was within an instant of getting into the car when he went down.

It was a surreal feeling. I kept saying: "He's just knocked out, isn't he?"

Hookesy's wife Robyn arrived and she was beside herself. We calmed her down and she rang her children, Caprice and Kristofer. Some time later, the doctor came into this room where Robyn, Mick Lewis, Lehmann, Phillips, Jackie Woodcock from 3AW and myself were waiting, and said something like: "There's no easy way to deliver this news. There's nothing we can do for him." He told us that Hookesy was in a coma, and that the life support system was keeping him alive, he was in fact brain dead. The situation was irretrievable.

There are no words that can convey the sense of disbelief and the sense of loss you feel at a time like this. Robyn went in to the room where Hookesy was laying, and Lehmann, Phillips, Jackie and I went with her. It must have been 3am or thereabouts, and other friends were arriving, like Gerard Healy, his close mate from 3AW.

Robyn needed support, and we stayed all night. When I headed home around 6am, I heard on the radio news: "David Hookes is fighting for his life in hospital …". We already knew that it was much worse than that.

* * *

That day, Cricket Victoria called in the players to give them the truth. For whatever reason, the media reports during the day had been overly optimistic. Shaun Graf told us that Hookesy wasn't fighting for his life, as had been reported. He wasn't coming back. They were keeping him on life support because he was an organ donor, and also to await the arrival of other members of his family.

It was a hell of a day. A lot of the players were distraught at the news. Some of them were going through the process of giving statements to the police, who were conducting inquiries. In the evening I caught up with a couple of media friends, Greg Baum and my co-author Martin Blake, at a pub in Richmond, and as I was driving home, Shane Warne rang me and said that he wanted to go to see Hookesy. The family said it would be okay, so Warney picked me up and we drove to the Alfred and were allowed in to see our coach at about midnight.

Paul Nobes, the former Victorian and South Australian batsman, had flown in from Adelaide and he came in as well. So did Gerard Healy and one or two others. We sat with him for 20 minutes. Warney was talking out loud to him and I held his hand with Robyn. We all let a few tears go. "We're going to win this for you mate. I know how much you wanted it," I said to him. It was a terribly sad and difficult time for everyone.

On the Tuesday, they turned off the life support.

We held a media conference at the Cricket Victoria offices near the MCG the next day. I asked that the whole squad be brought in to show our solidarity. Certain players were distraught, notably Robbie Cassell, who'd been with Hookesy when the incident occurred, and held his head as he lay on the road. Robbie was only 20. It was very traumatic for him. Mick Lewis also was doing it tough, along with Jon Moss and David Hussey, the guys who Hookesy had helped so much.

As captain, I read a prepared statement in which I gave Hookesy the best tribute I could muster. Needless to say, it was a tough thing to get through. Lehmann and I told Cricket Victoria that we couldn't play the scheduled Pura Cup game in Melbourne; that there was no way that the players would be ready.

They gave Hookesy an enormous funeral at Adelaide Oval. It was another emotionally-draining day, but it provided us some closure. We headed to a pub near the oval and a lot of his friends and teammates were there. People were still shocked at what had happened, but at least there had been a celebration of his life.

"I'm not here for a long time. I'm here for a good time," he used to say. Sadly, tragically, he was right about that one.

CHAPTER 17 BEST OF THE BEST

These teams are bound to cause some comment but they're my teams, so I have the final say. The first thing I need to explain is that I'm in the Victorian team, and you will have to excuse this indulgence. In 15 years, I never once played with another keeper so I don't have a lot of options! Suffice to say that this Victorian team is the one I want alongside me to go into battle.

The team is weighted to state cricket, which explains why, for instance, the Waugh brothers are not in the hybrid interstate team I have picked. Darren Lehmann's absence from the Victorian team, despite the fact he played a couple of seasons for the Vics, is because I regard him as a South Australian primarily. You will see that I have him in my interstate team, for I have the utmost respect for him.

These are the people and players I admired most from close range, beginning with the Victorian team:

Wayne Phillips is going to open the batting. Phillips was the quintessential quiet achiever, a guy who could play quick bowling so well that he extracted a century on debut against the West Indians when they were still a world force. Phillips was gutsy and I guess the fact he was involved in that match-winning partnership with Jamie Siddons in the 1990/91 Sheffield Shield final sticks in my mind. He wins one opening berth narrowly ahead of Gary Watts.

Matthew Elliott has been the outstanding opening batsman I played alongside, and he wins the other berth at the top of the order. Elliott to me was on a par with Matthew Hayden and it is a pity that he has not played more Test matches for Australia. Elliott can bat for long periods and he has matured as a person and a player. Early in his career there is no doubt his temperament was questionable. He was too moody and could be inconsistent in his approach. But in latter years I believe he became a more rounded person, particularly when he became a father, and it reflected in his cricket. He became more of a team man and when David Saker left Victoria to play in Tasmania, I anointed Elliott to lead the team song after our victories. Adding to the package, he is a very good second-slipper.

I didn't have any problems picking my No. 3 batsman. **Dean Jones** was a magnificent player both for Victoria and Australia over a long period and he deserves that position. As is well-documented, I had my ups and downs with Deano on a personal level. When I started we roomed together and he was helpful to me, which made our falling out in 1995 so difficult. Deano was a Jeckyl and Hyde figure in some ways. He could be very selfish at times and that may well have cost him a few Test matches. Having said that, he will be the star batsman in this line-up. He was tough, he never shirked, he worked harder on his game than any batsman I played with, he was absolutely meticulous at training and he was the complete player.

My No. 4 batsman won me over in recent years. **Brad Hodge** made 991 runs in his first season in state cricket when he was still sleeping in bunks at his parents' home with a poster of Dean Jones on his wall. He was a little kid and it took him seven or eight years to grow up. What I love about him is that at times, he is still that little kid. But the guy has been made captain of Leicestershire in England, which goes to show how much he's matured. On his day, he can bat as well as anyone. In his early days, he was dreadful against spin, but nowadays he smashes the slow bowlers. His elevation to the touring team for India this year was long overdue.

I'm asking **Jamie Siddons** to captain my team and bat at five. I loved playing with Siddons, and I regard the Victorian Cricket Association's failure to hold him here, allowing him to cross the border to South Australia not long after we had won the Shield, as one of the biggest mistakes it made. Siddons was not only an outstanding player; he was a fine captain who could have led Victoria for six or seven years. Instead the VCA went to Simon O'Donnell and then Dean Jones and we spent a few years struggling for success. I was always a believer that the state captain should be around all the time, like Stuart Law in Queensland. Siddons could have filled that more permanent role, presuming that the selectors weren't about to pick him at national level. He was the best fieldsman I played with, a brilliant slip catch, superb in-close and blessed with an amazing arm. In my first year with Victoria, he made two double-centuries and a match-winning hundred in the final.

Simon O'Donnell was a match-winner and captained the first of my two national championships so I've included him as the all-rounder, batting at No. 6. O'Donnell had played AFL football for St Kilda and he was a natural. I'll never forget him hitting Greg Matthews into the second level of the Great Southern Stand one day. Another time he walked out to bat in a bad mood – when he was captain he'd often be in a bad mood – and smashed one of the quickest centuries ever against New South Wales. He had his faults. He couldn't catch at slip, in fact he couldn't catch a cold in the South Pole and he only stood at slip because he thought the captain should. But as skipper of that Shield triumph he is going to edge out Tony Dodemaide in the all-rounder's spot. Dodemaide, who taught me so much, is in my 12 putting pressure on for a place. I must have him there after he bowled us both into the Shield final in 1990-91, then helped win the final for us as well with five second-innings wickets against New South Wales.

I batted ahead of **Paul Reiffel** when we played together but he's going up to No. 7 in my team. Reiffel earned his reputation as a nagging seamer but his batting was underestimated. I'd be happy with him at No. 7. Pistol was another one of those quiet, efficient players and he took more wickets for Victoria than anyone, which assures him of a game here. Even-tempered, he was a little misunderstood in a way. Just because he didn't say much didn't mean he didn't care or that he wasn't a team man. Pistol was always one of the last to leave the bar, win, lose or draw.

As strange as this may sound, **Shane Warne** could be considered a controversial selection. Warney's record for Australia is far better than it is for Victoria. But I'm simply not picking a Victorian team without the best cricketer I played with or against. My old mate will have to slot in behind me in the batting order, notwithstanding the fact he fancies himself with the bat. The other spinner I considered was Craig Howard, who came into the side at 19 and took a lot of wickets. Howard had the best wrong 'un I've seen, much better than Warne's, a spitting thing, but he wasn't nurtured by the team management and he dropped out of the side, which was a real shame.

Merv Hughes was the heart and soul of Victorian cricket for a long time, it's as simple as that. Hughes was the comedian of the team but at the same time, the bloke who tried the hardest. In that sense, he could be a contradiction. I recall him bowling a full

My greatest catch – baby Jordan.

© The Herald & Weekly Times Photographic Collection

"The Barrel" – My mentor and friend, the late John Scholes.

© The Herald & Weekly Times Photographic Collection

At the Junction Oval with David Hookes after being made the new captain of Victoria.

Celebrations after 'The Great Chase'. We needed 455 runs to beat NSW in Newcastle.
This was David Hookes' last Pura Cup game as Coach.

Celebrations begin! Joe Dawes caught Berry bowled Lewis to secure the Pura Cup 2003-04.

It doesn't get any better than this.

*Raw emotion.Coach Greg Shipperd embraces me moments after my
Pura Cup acceptance speech in which I also announced my retirement.*

© Gary Sparke

The Hookes philosophy: "We can win from anywhere".

How's this for a hat-trick. My wife Katherine, daughter Jordan, and the Pura Cup.

The Berry family at our wedding in April 1997.

Married to Katherine Bowes on April 19th, 1997.

*My beautiful baby girl
Jordan Olivia was born on
18th October, 2003.*

© The Herald & Weekly Times Photographic Collection

*Blowing a kiss to David Hookes' wife Robyn in the
stands at the MCG just days after David's death.*

session in Hobart on a flat track one day, and I'll never forget him bowling Western Australia out with six wickets in unbelievably hot conditions in Perth in our 1990/91 Shield-winning season. Merv was a great team man. Heaven forbid if you went to war, you'd want him with you.

My last pick is difficult but I'm going for **Mathew Inness** as the third paceman. I know people will throw up other names, and I considered Damien Fleming and David Saker for this spot. But with Hughes and Reiffel along with O'Donnell already in the team, all right-armers, I want a left-arm bowler. Inness also is a genuine swing bowler, as opposed to the pace of Hughes and the seam-up of Reiffel. Inness is the most successful fast bowler for Victoria since the Second World War. Prior to the 2004/05 season he had accumulated 199 wickets at 24 apiece and he's won many games for us, and taken a hat-trick. He's also vies with Dodemaide as the hardest-working bowler I've played with. If Inness came from New South Wales he would have played for Australia by now.

A thousand apologies are due to players who missed this team. Laurie Harper, a left-hander who averaged 36 for Victoria and who fielded superbly at slip alongside me, is unlucky. So is Warren Ayres, technically one of the best batsmen I've seen, who had to sit behind Jones, Hodge and Siddons. Ian Harvey could easily have won the all-rounder's spot, but ultimately his record does not quite stack up with O'Donnell's or Dodemaide's, at least not yet.

Now it's a matter of picking an opposition team. Once again, these are weighted along personal lines. They include a few players whom myself and Victoria had particular trouble with.

Jamie Cox of Tasmania can open the batting. Cox and I were roommates on the tour of the West Indies many years ago, and academy classmates. He always played well against Victoria.

Well-organised and calm, he should have been given a chance at the next level, and is due to break John Inverarity's long-standing games record for Sheffield Shield-Pura Cup during the 2004/05 season.

Matthew Hayden, the burly Queenslander, fills the other spot. Hayden destroyed Victoria over the years, long before the national selectors decided he was a world class player. I'll never forget one double-century he took off us in Brisbane when his power was just awesome. I always knew he would make it in Test cricket. It was a matter of getting the opportunity.

I don't know what **James Brayshaw** had against Victoria or Victorians, but it's a fact that of his eleven first class centuries for South Australia, six were against the Vics. We probably approached it the wrong way with Brayshaw, who was a pretty boy. We tried too hard, and Merv wanted to kill him. The results show that he had the game worked out.

Darren Lehmann and Jamie Siddons were the two stand-out Shield batsman of my time, and Lehmann wins a place in this hybrid team. Lehmann can hit balls to places and leave you wondering how in hell he did it. Watching him bat reminds me of the days when David Hookes would smash Peter Sleep's leg-spinners with the edge of his bat. It's exceptional talent, and Lehmann should have played more Test cricket. 'Boof' would be my choice to lead the team as he is very popular amongst his peers and is a top class skipper.

Michael Bevan was a guy who held up Victoria so many times, and I will have him at No. 5. If we had the firepower in our side, I always felt that we could get Bevan out with a couple of gullies in place. But if Merv Hughes wasn't playing or the quicks were away, we struggled. Bevan was a timer and worker of the ball but so often, you'd walk off and he'd be 60 not out, on the way to a big score. He annoyed us, rather than destroying us.

Tasmania's laconic all-rounder **Shaun 'China' Young** was a much-maligned player and will bat at six for this team. His body language was poor and he walked around as though everything was an effort. But he was dynamite when he got the bat or ball in his hands and played more than 100 games for Tassy. He was a brilliant state cricketer.

I had to choose between **Greg Matthews** and Tim May for the spinner's spot, and Matthews' batting got him in ahead of May. Plus I recall in my early days, Matthews got me out for fun. He'd bring in a bat-pad, I'd nick it and then I'd hear: "Seeya next time, Chux!" Not many spin bowlers can intimidate a batsman, but in state cricket, Matthews did. He was all over you. I loved his passion for the game and the cap he was wearing.

The wicketkeeper's spot in my best opposition team goes to **Peter Anderson**, who was an inspiration to me in the early part of my career. He was a clone of Allan Knott, the great English keeper. He simply had the best hands of any keeper I saw in Australian domestic cricket. Special mention goes to Mark Atkinson who was a tiny guy but a pure wicketkeeper. Atkinson had really good hands, and he was a hard worker. He was good up to the stumps, and he could make some dismissals standing up to the likes of Shaun Young and the quicker bowlers for Tasmania. Wade Seccombe, Tim Zoehrer and and Phil Emery, were all in the mix.

It's common knowledge that Victoria's nightmares begin at the Gabba in Brisbane. We took some ritual hammerings there early in the season and **Andy Bichel** was a big part of that. Bichel and Michael Kasprowicz among others were terribly tough on that seaming pitch. But I picked Bichel because he's one of my most admired players. He'd try to kill you then you'd walk off the ground and everything was fine. He played cricket the way I liked to play it.

I didn't play all that many games against Western Australian teams that included **Bruce Reid**, and that may have been a good thing for my average. I found the gigantic left-armer impossible to play. Everything he bowled hit the splice of the bat. I played against him at the WACA Ground once when there were massive cracks in the wicket, and he was pitching outside my leg-stump and coming in at my chest. It was terrifying.

My first game at first class level left me with an image of **Carl Rackemann**. Carl was a terrific guy but he bowled at your heart and he did it ball-after-ball, day-after-day. He never gave you a ball to drive. Batting against the Queenslander, you had no idea how to score. In my early days at least I was too scared to hook, and there was nothing to drive. The best I could muster would be a deflection to get off strike and a sigh of relief.

I popped the New South Welshman **Brad McNamara** in as 12th man for a couple of reasons. One is that he is widely regarded as the best "tourist" in the game. 'Buzzard' McNamara loves a beer and is great company. The second reason is that for a period, he got me out for fun. It was during a time when the MCG pitch was slow and low and McNamara bowled little medium-pace skidders. They'd throw him the ball as soon as I came in, I knew what to expect, but I couldn't keep him out.

VICTORIAN TEAM:

1 Wayne Phillips
2 Matthew Elliott
3 Dean Jones
4 Brad Hodge
5 Jamie Siddons (c)
6 Simon O'Donnell
7 Paul Reiffel
8 Darren Berry
9 Shane Warne
10 Merv Hughes
11 Mathew Inness
   Tony Dodemaide
   (12th man)

INTERSTATE TEAM:

1 Jamie Cox (Tas)
2 Matthew Hayden (Qld)
3 James Brayshaw (SA)
4 Darren Lehmann (SA)
5 Michael Bevan (NSW)
6 Shaun Young (Tas)
7 Greg Matthews (NSW)
8 Peter Anderson (Qld)
9 Andrew Bichel (Qld)
10 Bruce Reid (WA)
11 Carl Rackemann (Qld)
   Brad McNamara (NSW)
   (12th man)

CHAPTER 18 RETIREMENT

I was fortunate enough to have 15 years of playing first class cricket in Australia and I can safely say that the last of those was the most tumultuous of all. A string of major events wore me down emotionally. The death of my mentor, John Scholes, during the pre-season training period devastated me. I'd been appointed captain of the Pura Cup team, and while I'd led the state before many times, previously it had always been on a fill-in basis when Shane Warne was absent. Then before I knew it, I'd suffered a serious finger injury in a trial game and required surgery, keeping me out of cricket for eight weeks just when I felt as though I needed to be around. I'd given up my place in the team, not the ideal result for a 33-year-old, let alone the newly-appointed captain. The birth of my first child in October, a beautiful daughter we named Jordan Olivia, utterly changed my perspective on life. Suddenly cricket didn't come first, second and third anymore. Then in January, with the team flying and me ready to resume playing, David Hookes' death shook our world to the foundations. Ultimately, of course, we would win the national championship under my captaincy and I chose that moment to end my career.

I always thought that I would play until I dropped. I just never pictured myself voluntarily moving on. I figured they'd get me before I had the chance to get out, and there was a certain amount of logic in this. Bob Taylor, the fine English keeper, had played well into his 40s and he was an inspiration to me. There'd also been Colin 'Funky' Miller, my old South Australian and Victorian teammate, who had to wait until he was 34 to get the baggy, green cap. Right up until near the end, I truly believed that I would play for Australia; that a door would open somewhere just as it opened for 'Funky'. But, as I've said, so much happened in that last season. In the end, I shocked myself by retiring. But I knew. I just knew it was time.

All through my career I prided myself on being the best wicketkeeper. I enjoyed practice and I gobbled up the hard work that was involved. But to be perfectly honest, after Christmas in that final season I was turning up and I no longer had it in me to do the extra work. Earlier, I'd get in behind the batsmen for 30 minutes of stumping; all those little things you undertake to make yourself the best at what you do. Now I was finding it a chore, rather than feeding a passion. The finger injury I'd suffered had required four pins and was still causing me some grief. I knew that to play on, I'd need to do another pre-season and cricketers don't get the luxury of a quiet pre-season anymore. There would be lots of running The Tan track and I didn't have it in me. Yes, I could have bluffed the system and played another couple of years. But that wasn't my style and I just knew I was ready to move on.

There's no doubt the emotional stress that built up from the deaths of Scholes and Hookes took their toll. Those events, and Jordan's birth, were important to the decision. Without being disrespectful to Kath, I would say that from the time I passed my HSC and left high school in Wonthaggi, I made cricket my life.

Now I was feeling like there was much more to be enjoyed and experienced. I'd discussed these things with Kath late in the season, but the final straw for me came after the incredibly stressful and emotional weeks around David Hookes' death.

One of the toughest jobs I've ever endured came in the days after our coach's death, when I was required to front a media conference in the Cricket Victoria board room and tell the rest of the world how the players were handling it. Remember that this was an event which was front-page news around the country, and there were dozens of media crammed into that room on the day. I was still terribly upset myself, and I'd been spending a lot of time helping some of the younger players get through the trauma. I arranged to have the whole squad attend the conference, to show that we were sticking together. Cameron White, the heir apparent and already the captain for one-day cricket, was beside me as well as Matthew Elliott, Jonathon Moss, and assistant coach Greg Shipperd. The others stood in a group behind us and I read from a prepared statement, struggling to get the words out without breaking down and blubbering.

But just after that media conference something happened that upset me. CV's Cricket Operations Manager, Shaun Graf, called me into his office and asked me to shut the door. I was still shaking and I was a mess. Graf said that he was "a bit concerned that this has become the Darren Berry media circus". He said that I needed to give Cameron White, as the future captain, an opportunity to handle some of these things. Graf and I had a love-hate relationship over the years. We respected each other, and he'd been a fine player and part of a Victorian Sheffield Shield victory. But there was plenty of angst between us at times. I always felt that he wanted to pull me down a peg or two. I know, also, that Graf was very close to Hookes and under pressure like the rest of us. But on this day, I was close to climbing over his desk and knocking him out.

"The kid (White) is 19 years old, do you really think he needs to be up there explaining how he feels about losing his coach?" I said: "If you think I wanted to do that, you've got rocks in your head." I was very upset and hurt by Graf's statement. I'd fronted the media conference as the state captain. I hadn't been in the media in the previous couple of days, other than writing a column for *The Age* as a tribute to Hookes, and that was at the newspaper's request. The idea that I was trying to make it my show was callous and downright disrespectful. A few of our players were really struggling emotionally, especially young Robbie Cassell. I knew full well that Victoria was grooming Cameron White to take on the captaincy on a long-term basis. It was Hookes' vision that it be so, and I was all for it.

The upcoming game against South Australia was cancelled out of respect for Hookes, but we stayed in Adelaide after our coach's funeral to play against SA and I was picked for my first game after the finger injury. Needless to say I was not ready and it went badly. I had a poor game, making a duck and 1 with the bat and failing to get a glove on a high catch that I would have swallowed normally. After my second-innings duck, all the emotion came tumbling out. Furious, I kept myself nice until I reached the dressing rooms up the top of the stairs in the grandstand at Adelaide Oval.

The rooms at Adelaide Oval are unusual in the sense that the players' viewing area has no glass front on it. It's just an open area with the actual dressing room area behind a partition at the rear. This was to prove costly for me. The build-up of frustration and anger and emotion got the best of me, and as I walked into the room, I hurled my bat into my pile of gear in the corner that had been mine for 15 years at Adelaide Oval. As I turned to sit down, I tripped over my bag and smashed my back into the lockers. Simultaneously, I yelled the loudest "Fuuuccckkk" I could possibly muster. It was so loud that I could hear one or two oohs and aahs from the spectators out in the grandstand.

We won the game outright, a mighty effort in the circumstances. But I was reported for uttering an audible obscenity and fined 25 percent of my match fee. One of the umpires told the hearing that he could hear me from out on the ground. I told them: "I'm sorry. I've had a tough 10 days. It's no excuse, but I did it, and I apologise." I thought that would be the end of the matter. I'd soured our win a little and I was embarrassed, but I knew that it had been the result of a couple of horrible weeks and that at least I'd kept my cool until I'd reached the (relative) privacy of the dressing room.

As it turned out, this was only the beginning of my problems. At 7.30 the next morning the phone in my hotel room rang. It was Graf, who'd sat in on the hearing the night before. He told me that the board of Cricket Victoria wanted to meet me when I returned to Melbourne. He said: "Did you talk to them about Spirit of Cricket at the start of the year?" I told him that I had. "Well they're not happy about you getting reported," he said. At this point I figured someone must have made a call to the hierarchy, how else would they have known so soon?

The Spirit of Cricket is an initiative of Cricket Australia aimed at improving the behaviour of players on and off the field, and it had filtered down through the state associations in the previous year. When I was appointed captain at the start of the season I'd had a meeting with the head honchos of CV, executive director Ken Jacobs, deputy-chairman Tony Steele, president Bob Merriman and chairman Geoff Tamblyn. It was a cordial meeting. They asked me if I could ensure that the players behaved in a manner that fitted in with the new philosophy and if

Victoria could improve its image, since in the previous season the umpires had rated us last of all the states in the behaviour stakes.

They wanted me to sign a document to say that I would toe the line for 12 months, but I wouldn't. My response was: "This is not under 12 cricket. If you want me to be captain, I'll give you my word, and I'll do it to the best of my ability. I understand what you're saying." Merriman said: "Ok. Your word's good enough for me, Chuck."

Hence, I knew when Graf rang me that I was headed for a tough time in Melbourne. Kath picked me up at the airport so I could go straight to the office, near the MCG, and when I walked in, Ken Jacobs and Geoff Tamblyn had very serious looks on their faces. We went into the board room and Tamblyn spoke about the Spirit of Cricket. He said I'd breached the agreement and that they would like me to resign from the captaincy. You could have knocked me down with a feather at this point. "No Tambo, I've never quit anything," I told him. "You'll have to sack me if you want me out." There was some to-and-fro after that. Tamblyn told me that the resignation could be presented in a professional manner, with me issuing a statement and backing up the Spirit of Cricket, acknowledging its importance. But I wouldn't cop it.

In my humble opinion, Cricket Victoria showed absolutely no compassion for me in this instance. They paid no mind to the fact that we'd all been to hell and back in the previous couple of weeks and they gave me no respect for the service I'd provided over 15 years. They were prepared to end the career of the state games record-holder right then and there because I dropped the F-word in the dressing room. What I did was wrong, and I don't condone it. But it had happened in the dressing room and at the end of an awful few weeks. That was the rub for me. If I'd sworn at an umpire on the field or made a public nuisance of myself, then I would have considered my position. But to me, the punishment was way out of whack with the crime. Not only that, it threatened to derail what was shaping as a brilliant season on the field. We were clear on top of the Pura Cup table at this point.

I tried to reason with them. "Forget about me," I said. "What about the team, after what they've been through with Hookesy? You're going to have: 'Berry resigns as captain' in the press. They're going to be all over it. Have you got any idea? We're on top of the ladder. This is going to be a major distraction." Tamblyn said: "We can handle that." I told them that I didn't believe it was about the Adelaide incident; that it couldn't be so simple. In the end, I just broke down in tears. I could see that Jacobs was uncomfortable, but Tamblyn was insistent. "Ken, I've known you for a long time and I respect you," I said. "Tambo, you were good to me when I was dropped in '95. I respect you. I can't believe what you're saying to me."

They told me they wanted me to continue playing, but not as captain. I refused. Ultimately Tamblyn said: "You've left us with no option but to sack you. We're going to have to go back to the board on this." I walked out in tears and began to piece the events together. I was annoyed with Graf, who had given the appearance of knowing nothing when he called me the previous morning. I learned later that Graf had been potting me to others in the bar the previous night, after I'd been fined.

Kath was supportive as we drove home that day but I was gutted to say the least. What followed were a couple of days of soul-searching. Jacobs contacted me and tried to get me to come back into the office to talk it through. I told him there was nothing to talk about, that if I was to be sacked then so be it. I didn't know who to ring about it, and I didn't tell anyone other than a couple of Wonthaggi friends and Kath. None of the players knew this. Then I rang Tim May, president of the players' union, the Australian Cricketers' Association, for some advice.

May got in touch with Tamblyn, and they held a meeting. I don't know the full details of what occurred, but from what I understand, May told Cricket Victoria that the ACA would support its player 100 percent in the circumstances and that CV would be hammered in the press for forcing the resignation of the captain at such a difficult time.

Ultimately, Tim May saved me. When it came to the crunch, they wouldn't sack me. They knew they'd be made to look uncharitable in the circumstances. CV came back to me with a compromise letter that I was required to sign. It said that if I was reported again I would lose the captaincy, and a match payment. I said that I would sign for the sake of the team, and I took the letter back to Jacobs the following day. By this time, the deferred match against South Australia was about to begin in Melbourne, and Bob Merriman came into the rooms before the game. Merriman, one of Australian cricket's powerbrokers for more than 20 years, took me into the medical room. I'd always respected him and he had been good to me throughout my career. He told me that the full board of CV was behind me. I looked at him and said: "Listen, don't look me in the eye and say that. I know they're not behind me." He said: "Don't be like that. It's been a difficult time, and you've got our support." We shook hands and I said I was going on for the sake of Victorian cricket. "Good to hear that," he said.

As I said, my near-sacking shook me to the core and near the end of what had already been a tough season, it tipped me over the edge. Once again, cricket politics had got the better of me. I began to think that I didn't want to be part of it any more.

* * *

Upon reflection, I am happy with my career, although disappointed I didn't play a Test match for Australia. Ultimately I averaged just under 23 for Victoria with the bat and that held me back, especially in the modern era where the authorities are seeking batsman-keepers rather than the reverse. I could bat okay, but I wasn't consistent enough. And I batted for the team, which meant that if we needed quick runs, I'd go for them. I could have been more selfish and pushed for the 25 or 30 not out, which I saw some guys do. But I didn't protect my average; it wasn't the way I played the game.

I was known as a very good keeper who could bat a bit, but that wasn't enough to push me to the next level. In another era it might well have been. In my 15 years, the Test wicketkeeping spot was filled for a decade by Ian Healy, and for the next five years by Adam Gilchrist, both champions. Had I come along a few years early, in that period when Wayne Phillips, Greg Dyer and Tim Zoehrer stood behind the stumps, none of them securing their position, then maybe I could have played for my country for a few years. But I'm not the first keeper to miss out in this way. Richie Robinson, another Victorian, sat behind Rodney Marsh for his whole career and Bob Taylor had to wait behind Alan Knott until he was 36 to play for England regularly.

Although other people wrote me off as a potential Test player, I'd kept the faith right to the end, right up until Australia named its team to make a tour of Sri Lanka in March, 2004. I knew that with so much cricket to be played, they would most likely take a second keeper to back-up Adam Gilchrist and that was the spot I was hoping for. I also knew that Shane Warne and Stuart MacGill would be the two spinners on that tour, and my history of keeping to Warne would help my cause, especially on spinning subcontinental strips.

When I didn't make that team, it got to me. They picked Wade Seccombe, the Queenslander who had little or no experience with leg-spinners. I ran into David Boon, the Test selector, in Melbourne and I put it on him as to why I'd missed out. I'd known Boony for a long time and the discussion was direct, without being aggressive. I told him that I couldn't understand the logic. Boony told me that my batting had cost me, plus the fact that I'd been out of cricket with my finger injury. It was at this point that finally I realised I was not on the radar for national selection. And that was crucial to my decision to retire from the game.

I understand the difficulties of selection and the only thing that irks me is that in all my time as a player, I never once got picked for Australia 'A' when plenty of other keepers did. I had a couple of gigs in the Prime Minister's XI and that was about it for those types of matches. My difficulties with Victorian cricket authorities left scars on me, but overall I'm very thankful for the opportunity they gave me to play and pursue my dream. I loved playing for Victoria, and it meant everything to me.

So what now? I'm looking forward to spending more time with my wife and daughter, doing things that cricketers never get to do. I'm going to the beach with the family on the weekends. I'm going to the Melbourne Cup, something I've always missed because club cricket has been played on Cup day. I'm going away from cricket for a while but I want to come back. When the time is right, I'd love to coach Victoria.

I'm calling football on radio for MMM, which is another passion. I'm also looking after a few young players with their contract negotiations in a mentor/manager type role that may well lead to a career down the track in player management.

Most of all I'm going to enjoy myself, and when I drive past a dusty cricket ground on a Sunday afternoon in the bush and I see the bloke squatting down behind the stumps, I'll think: "That's what I did for 25 years."

EPILOGUE   THE FINAL WORD

BY KATHERINE BERRY

They say opposites attract, and in our case they are right. Where Darren is spontaneous, I am cautious. Where he is impatient, I am tolerant and where he is gregarious, I am reserved. We've often remarked how different our childhood experiences have been. Circa 1978 on a Saturday night, for him it was watching 'Seven's Big League'. For me it was 'Young Talent Time'. If you had asked me then what my least favourite sport was, the answer would have been cricket. How ironic that I married a cricketer.

Having no understanding of cricket was perhaps a good thing initially, because by the time I did understand it and realised the enormity of focus and commitment he was willing to devote to his sport, it was too late. I was head over heels and there was no turning back. Cricket was part of the package. So rather than compete with it, I chose to accept it and the unusual lifestyle that it brought, and what it allowed me to do was develop a sense of independence and put energy into my own career, while allowing Darren to chase his dream unencumbered.

It's so appropriate that Darren played a team sport because he is easily bored with his own company. The camaraderie and shenanigans of his teammates has given him great pleasure over the years. He loves the social interaction of spending time with others and meeting new people. He has that special ability to walk into a room of complete strangers and strike up a conversation, have a blast of a time and be one of the last ones to leave, complete with some new acquaintances who are well on their way to becoming established friends.

It's that 'gift of the gab', knowing the right things to say and when, coming out with those quick 'one liners' and being able to think on his feet. I remember once going to a 21st party where upon entering the room, Darren was asked to make an impromptu speech. While the thought of public speaking with no notice would send panic waves through most people, Darren obliged, made his way amongst the 80 or so guests to the front of the room, reeled off a warm and thoughtful speech, threw in a couple of appropriately funny lines and managed to bring the house down at the same time. It's this quality that others of all ages warm to, and it's one of the many things I love about him.

For someone so comfortable with spontaneity, Darren spends an incredible amount of time planning all that he does in life. He and his diary are inseparable. He records all sorts of details in there and as a result, never misses an appointment or meeting and always remembers to send birthday cards. Even in the early days, while most young cricketers were enjoying the moment, getting paid to play the sport they love, Darren was already thinking about life after cricket. He enrolled himself in a Bachelor of Applied Science degree, and although with cricket commitments it took him eight years to complete, he did it and is now a qualified PE secondary teacher, the degree hanging proudly on the wall.

There's always a quirky thing about your partner that you often tease them about but secretly find great humour in, and I think it would be remiss of me not to share it at this time. Darren is obsessively tidy. The Vic boys can attest to his neatness with his cricket belongings. Apparently he is the only Victorian cricketer to have taken the time each game to place his four days worth of whites on coat hangers and hang them in his locker. On interstate trips, many a roommate has taken great delight in messing up his things, much to Darren's annoyance. This tidiness extends to our home as well. His wardrobe is impeccable; it replicates the standards of a high quality department store. That's not to say that he doesn't leave things lying around. He does, but in neat orderly piles, hence the nickname 'Gomer' has stuck over the years. It's become such a habit that he isn't even aware he is doing it half the time. I recently watched him talking on the phone while simultaneously aligning the sauce bottles in the pantry. Freaky – but loveable all the same and I never have to tidy up after him!

I can see how people would perceive Darren as having an air of confidence about him and certainly to succeed in any sport you need to have confidence and belief in your own ability. Yet beneath the surface is a sensitive man that only a privileged few get to see. A man who lost both his parents at a young age and a man who has endured the loss of several people very close to him. As a cricketer he has exuded a tough exterior, but has been stung and genuinely hurt by some of the decisions and actions of colleagues and administrators over the years. He has shown great courage and leadership in these times and as I look back at this, I am immensely proud of him. I believe it's the knocks and setbacks in life that shape you, and for Darren, this has only served to make him stronger. He embraces all that he does in life with a high level of intensity and passion — there are no half measures. It's 110% or nothing at all. He is an amazing person to be around and a true inspiration if you are ever feeling sorry or unsure in life.

For as long as Darren and I have been together, he has always been a cricketer. It has been a consuming sport and not without its politics. Yet, it has also allowed us to travel all over the world, meet all kinds of interesting people and make some life long friends, and for that I am grateful to the game.

Retirement is not an easy decision, and for Darren it was a case of the heart wanting to go on but the head saying otherwise. While an Australian Test match was never attained, he walks away from the game knowing he gave Victorian cricket his all. Records were broken and championships were won, however his best performance by far is one not recorded in any stats book.

It's his role as a 'Dad' and in this he is a star performer. To watch him with Jordan is a pure delight and she is quite obviously his pride and joy and a nice distraction from cricket. There's something about seeing a tough competitor speak in baby talk that melts your heart. I look forward to a somewhat normal life, spending summers with my husband and daughter at the beach, the MCG nowhere in sight. However, I'm a realist and I know deep down that sooner or later the game of cricket will beckon him back in some form or another and knowing the Darren Berry that I know, he won't be able to resist.

CAREER STATISTICS

Berry, Darren Shane
Born: December 10, 1969
Wicketkeeper – Right-hand Batsman

First Class Debut:
1989-90 South Australia v Queensland at the Gabba

DARREN BERRY CAREER STATISTICS

	M	I	NO	HS	R	Ave	Ct	St	Dis
First Class	153	231	33	166*	4273	21.5	552	51	603
Sheffield Shield/ Pura Cup	139	212	30	166*	3963	21.7	499	47	546

VICTORIAN CAREER

	M	I	NO	HS	R	Ave	Ct	St	Dis
First Class	138	212	31	166*	4077	22.5	510	47	557
Sheffield Shield/ Pura Cup	129	198	29	166*	3816	22.5	468	44	512
One Day	87	66	21	64*	814	18.0	105	30	135
District Cricket	131	111	18	128	3149	33.8	175	34	209

CAPTAINCY RECORD

First Class	27 Games	14 Wins	6 Losses	7 Draws	52%
Sheffield Shield/ Pura Cup	25 Games	12 Wins	6 Losses	7 Draws	48%
One Day	20 Games	9 Wins	10 Losses	1 N/R	45%

Legend:

M - Matches	I - Innings	NO - Not Out
HS - Highest Score	Ave - Average	Ct - Catches
St - Stumpings	Dis - Dismissals	R - Runs
Ttl - Total	Bwd - Bowled	Cfd - Caught fielder
Cwk - Caught keeper	RO - Run Out	HW - Hit wicket
HB - Handled ball		

SHEFFIELD SHIELD/PURA CUP CAREER
MOST WICKETKEEPING DISMISSALS

Name	M	R	Ave	W	Ave	Ct	St	Dis
DS Berry	139	3963	21.77	0	-	499	47	546
WA Seccombe	93	2952	25.89	0	-	437	12	449
TJ Zoehrer	107	4248	30.78	23	58.30	331	28	359
RW Marsh	86	4412	33.93	0	-	318	33	351
PA Emery	109	3081	25.67	0	-	298	41	339
JA Maclean	86	3277	25.20	0	-	290	24	314
TJ Nielsen	92	3531	26.15	0	-	257	29	286
ATW Grout	86	3049	23.63	0	-	213	63	276
AC Gilchrist	60	3196	38.97	-	-	260	8	268
MN Atkinson	84	2350	29.01	-	-	237	25	262
SJ Rixon	94	3008	26.38	-	-	218	41	259
BN Jarman	77	2984	24.86	0	-	192	58	250
RD Robinson	68	3407	39.16	-	-	212	26	238
RB Phillips	71	2271	26.10	-	-	221	11	232
RC Jordon	70	2006	26.05	-	-	199	31	230
KJ Wright	63	2095	29.92	-	-	197	17	214
HB Taber	64	1377	16.59	-	-	179	32	211
D Tallon	69	3594	30.71	0	-	145	61	206
CW Walker	57	1002	13.72	-	-	103	87	190
RJ Campbell	71	4496	37.15	0	-	175	8	183
WAS Oldfield	51	1790	25.21	-	-	109	70	179
MGD Dimattina	60	1305	20.71	0	-	149	19	168
PW Anderson	53	1342	18.38	0	-	152	14	166
IA Healy	45	1859	37.93	0	-	158	7	165

MOST FIRST-CLASS GAMES FOR ONE STATE

Player		Career	Games
J Cox	Tas	1987-88 - 2003-04	163
SG Law	QLD	1988-89 - 2003-04	158
PR Sleep	SA	1976-77 - 1992-93	146
TM Moody	WA	1985-86 - 2000-01	145
LE Favell	SA	1951-52 - 1969-70	143
DC Boon	Tas	1978-79 - 1998-99	139
DS Berry	Vic	1990-91 - 2003-04	138
DW Hookes	SA	1975-76 - 1991-92	136
GRJ Matthews	NSW	1982-83 - 1997-98	135
SC Trimble	Qld	1959-60 - 1975-76	133

MOST FIRST-CLASS APPEARANCES FOR VICTORIA

Player	Career	Games
DS Berry	1990-91 - 2003-04	138
DM Jones	1981-82 - 1997-98	124
RJ Bright	1972-73 - 1987-88	114
AIC Dodemaide	1983-84 - 1997-98	105
BJ Hodge	1993-94 - 2003-04	104
WM Lawry	1955-56 - 1971-72	99
DF Whatmore	1975-76 - 1988-89	95
MTG Elliott	1992-93 - 2003-04	97
IR Redpath	1961-62 - 1975-76	92
PR Reiffel	1987-88 - 2001-02	92

MOST FIRST-CLASS DISMISSALS BY WICKETKEEPERS FOR VICTORIA

Wicketkeeper	M	Total	Ct	St
DS Berry	139	557	510	47
RD Robinson	76	265	235	30
RC Jordon	79	260	226	34
JL Ellis	72	202	146	56
MGD Dimattina	67	188	167	21

FIRST-CLASS PARTNERSHIP RECORDS FOR VICTORIA

Wkt	Ttl	Batsmen	Versus	Venue	Season
1st	456	WH Ponsford & RE Mayne	Qld	Melb	1923-24
2nd	358	HHL Kortlang & C McKenzie	WA	Perth	1909-10
3rd	390*	JM Wiener & JK Moss	WA	St Kilda	1981-82
4th	424	IS Lee & SO Quin	Tas	Melb	1933-34
5th	343	RI Maddocks & J Hallebone	Tas	Melb	1951-52
6th	290	MTG Elliott & **DS Berry**	NSW	Sydney	1996-97
7th	187	PA McAlister & AW Murray	NZ	Melb	1898-99
8th	215	WW Armstrong & RL Park	SA	Melb	1919-20
9th	146	TS Warne & AC Facy	Tas	Laun.	1911-12
10th	211	M Ellis & TJ Hastings	SA	Melb	1902-03

MOST APPEARANCES IN THE SHEFFIELD SHIELD/ PURA CUP

Player	State	Career	Games
RJ Inverarity	WA-SA	1962-63 - 1984-85	159
J Cox	Tas	1987-88 - 2003-04	153
JD Siddons	Vic-SA	1984-85 - 1999-00	146
SG Law	Qld	1988-89 - 2003-04	142
DS Berry	SA-Vic	1989-90 - 2003-04	139
TM Moody	WA	1985-86 - 2000-01	132
PR Sleep	SA	1976-77 - 1992-93	127
DS Lehmann	SA-Vic	1987-88 - 2003-04	125
SC Trimble	Qld	1959-60 - 1975-76	123
LE Favell	SA	1951-52 - 1969-70	120
DW Hookes	SA	1975-76 - 1991-92	120

MOST SHEFFIELD SHIELD/PURA CUP APPEARANCES FOR VICTORIA

Player	Career	Games
DS Berry	1990-91 - 2003-04	129
DM Jones	1981-82 - 1997-98	110
RJ Bright	1972-73 - 1987-88	101
BJ Hodge	1993-94 - 2003-04	98
AIC Dodemaide	1983-84 - 1997-98	94
MTG Elliott	1992-93 - 2003-04	93
PR Reiffel	1987-88 - 2001-02	86
WM Lawry	1955-56 - 1971-72	85
DF Whatmore	1975-76 - 1988-89	85
GN Yallop	1972-73 - 1984-85	76
MG Hughes	1981-82 - 1994-95	76
IR Redpath	1961-62 - 1975-76	76

MOST SHEFFIELD SHIELD/PURA CUP DISMISSALS BY WICKETKEEPERS FOR VICTORIA

Wicketkeeper	M	Total	Ct	St
DS Berry	129	512	468	44
RD Robinson	68	238	212	26
RC Jordan	70	230	199	31
MGD Dimattina	60	168	149	19
JL Ellis	49	156	111	45

SHEFFIELD SHIELD/PURA CUP PARTNERSHIP RECORDS FOR VICTORIA

Wkt	Ttl	Batsmen	Versus	Venue	Season
1st	375	WM Woodfull & WH Ponsford	NSW	Melb	1926-27
2nd	314	WH Ponsford & HSTL Hendry	Qld	St Kilda	1927-28
3rd	390*	JM Wiener & JK Moss	WA	St Kilda	1981-82
4th	309*	J Moss & DJ Hussey	WA	Perth	2003-04
5th	316*	LD Harper & GB Gardiner	SA	Carlton	1997-98
6th	290	MTG Elliott & **DS Berry**	NSW	Sydney	1996-97
7th	185	PA Hibbert & RJ Bright	NSW	Melb	1985-86
8th	215	WW Armstrong & RL Park	SA	Melb	1919-20
9th	143	GR Hazlitt & A Kenny	SA	Melb	1910-11
10th	211	M Ellis & TJ Hastings	SA	Melb	1902-03

AUSTRALIAN DOMESTIC LIMITED-OVERS FASTEST FIFTIES

Balls	Player	Game	Season
21	DW Hookes	South Australia v Western Australia at Adelaide	1990-91
24	DA Nash	New South Wales v Western Australia at North Sydney	2000-01
26	SG Law	Queensland v Tasmania at Hobart (Bel)	2003-04
27	IJ Harvey	Victoria v Tasmania at Hobart (Bel)	1998-99
28	**DS Berry**	Victoria v New South Wales at North Sydney	1997-98
29	GA Manou	South Australia v Tasmania at Adelaide	2002-03
30	MG Bevan	New South Wales v Victoria at Sydney	1992-93
31	RW Marsh	Western Australia v South Australia at Adelaide	1983-84
31	BJ Hodge	Victoria v Tasmania at Hobart (Bel)	1998-99
31	MA Higgs	New South Wales v Queensland at Sydney	2001-02
31	PA Jaques	New South Wales v Tasmania at Sydney	2003-04

AUSTRALIAN DOMESTIC LIMITED-OVERS MOST APPEARANCES

Player	Team	Career	Games
DS Berry	SA-Vic	1989-90 - 2003-04	87
SG Law	Qld	1988-89 - 2003-04	85
GS Blewett	SA	1992-93 - 2003-04	79
JL Langer	WA	1992-93 - 2003-04	78
ML Love	Qld	1993-94 - 2003-04	78
TM Moody	WA	1985-86 - 2000-01	75
J Cox	Tas	1988-89 - 2003-04	75
BJ Hodge	Vic	1993-94 - 2003-04	75
MJ Di Venuto	Tas	1997-98 - 2003-04	75
DS Lehmann	SA-Vic	1988-89 - 2003-04	75
J Angel	WA	1992-93 - 2003-04	74

AUSTRALIAN DOMESTIC LIMITED-OVERS MOST DISMISSALS BY A WICKETKEEPER IN A CAREER

Wicketkeeper		M	Ttl	Ct	St
DS Berry	SA-Vic	87	134	105	29
WA Seccombe	Qld	69	112	92	20
BJ Haddin	ACT-NSW	51	92	73	19
RJ Campbell	WA	46	86	80	6
PA Emery	NSW	58	81	70	11
AC Gilchrist	NSW-WA	36	70	64	6
GA Manou	SA	45	62	59	3
TJ Nielsen	SA	45	57	54	3
IA Healy	Qld	29	54	47	7
RW Marsh	WA	33	52	51	1
MN Atkinson	Tas	35	50	43	7

FIRST CLASS CAREER

Season	Country	M	Inn	NO	Runs	HS	0s	50	100	Ave	Ct	St
1989-90	Australia	12	16	2	171	38	3	-	-	12.21	32	3
1990-91	Australia	12	16	2	305	98	3	1	-	21.79	48	-
1991	England	1	2	-	5	4	-	-	-	2.50	1	1
1991-92	Australia	11	12	1	190	49	-	-	-	17.27	43	6
1992-93	Australia	10	15	4	182	57	-	1	-	16.55	31	4
1993	England	1	1	-	4	4	-	-	-	4.00	1	-
1993-94	Australia	11	18	5	184	38*	3	-	-	14.15	37	6
1994-95	Australia	11	18	1	399	55	2	1	-	23.47	45	3
1995-96	Australia	4	6	1	161	74	-	1	-	32.20	18	2
1996-97	Australia	11	20	1	590	148	3	2	1	31.05	40	5
1997	England	2	2	-	21	12	-	-	-	10.50	9	1
1997-98	Australia	11	19	3	440	166*	2	-	1	27.50	39	6
1998-99	Australia	10	16	4	181	31	3	-	-	15.08	36	2
1999-00	Australia	11	16	3	390	106	3	1	1	30.00	52	2
2000-01	Australia	10	17	1	230	61	2	1	-	14.38	36	1
2001-02	Australia	10	16	3	382	148	2	1	1	29.38	32	3
2002-03	Australia	9	14	1	299	52	-	1	-	23.00	32	3
2003-04	Australia	6	7	1	139	61	2	1	-	23.17	20	3
Total		**153**	**231**	**33**	**4273**	**166***	**28**	**11**	**4**	**21.58**	**552**	**51**

Opponents	M	Inn	N.O	Runs	HS	0s	50	100	Ave	Ct	St
Essex	1	2	-	5	4	-	-	-	2.50	1	1
England XI	2	4	1	100	47*	1	-	-	33.33	5	-
Glamorgan	1	1	-	9	9	-	-	-	9.00	3	1
Kent	1	1	-	12	12	-	-	-	12.00	6	-
New South Wales	27	41	8	1011	166*	1	1	4	30.64	89	9
New Zealanders	2	3	1	36	27	-	-	-	18.00	8	-
Pakistanis	2	2	-	54	49	-	-	-	27.00	17	2
Queensland	30	52	4	791	74	9	3	-	16.48	118	8
South Australia	26	36	7	548	52	4	1	-	18.90	104	12
South Africans	1	1	-	0	0	1	-	-	0.00	5	-
Sri Lankans	1	1	1	17	17+	-	-	-	-	-	-
Tasmania	28	39	6	825	98	4	3	-	25.00	87	9
Victoria	2	3	-	23	17	1	-	-	7.67	5	1
Western Australia	26	41	5	765	83	6	2	-	21.25	96	8
West Indians	2	3	-	73	50	1	1	-	24.33	7	-
Zimbabweans	1	1	-	4	4	-	-	-	4.00	1	-

CAREER BY TEAM

Team	M	Inn	NO	Runs	HS	0s	50	100	Ave	Ct	St
Australian XI	2	2	-	21	12	-	-	-	10.50	9	1
South Australia	12	16	2	171	38	3	-	-	12.21	32	3
Victoria	138	212	31	4077	166*	25	11	4	22.52	510	47
World XI	1	1	-	4	4	-	-	-	4.00	1	-

HOW DISMISSED

Inns	NO	Bwd	Cfd	Cwk	LBW	St	RO	HW	HB
231	33	28	89	49	23	6	3	-	-

HIGHEST SCORES

Score	Game	Venue	Season
166*	Vic v NSW	Melbourne	1997-98
148	Vic v NSW	SCG	1996-97
148	Vic v NSW	SCG	2001-02
106	Vic v NSW	Punt Rd Oval	1999-2000

FIRST-CLASS CAPTAINCY RECORD

	Capt	Win	Loss	Draw	Tie	% Won
New South Wales	3	2	-	1	-	66.67
New Zealanders	1	1	-	-	-	100.00
Queensland	5	2	3	-	-	40.00
South Australia	6	4	-	2	-	66.67
Tasmania	6	2	2	2	-	33.33
Western Australia	5	2	1	2	-	40.00
West Indians	1	1	-	-	-	100.00
Total	**27**	**14**	**6**	**7**	**-**	**51.85**

ABOUT THE CO-AUTHOR

Martin Blake was born in Stawell in western Victoria and grew up within a stone's throw of Central Park, home of the famous Stawell Easter Gift foot race. He played cricket and football and other sports in Victorian country areas and has been a journalist for 25 years, the past 18 of those at *The Age* in Melbourne. He has covered cricket in most parts of the world including Australia's World Cup wins in India in 1987 and England in 1999, as well as the Ashes tour of 1989 when Allan Border's team brought the famous trophy home to Australia. He has also covered several Olympic Games, Commonwealth Games and numerous AFL seasons. He has been a friend of Darren Berry's for a decade.